M000200934

7000467875

35314

BUILDING
HAPPINESS
ARCHITECTURE TO MAKE YOU SMILE

EDITED BY JANE WERNICK
RIBA BUILDING FUTURES

UWE. Bristol

17 FEB 2009
BNE
Library Services

black dog
publishing
london uk

CONTENTS

INTRODUCTION

JANE WERNICK

Attaining a state of happiness has been seen as a goal since ancient times, and surely in today's conflicted world, we all yearn for inner peace and happiness? The Eastern definitions of happiness imply that it is a state that lies within us and cannot be provided by others. It is seen as a trancing state, because often we are at our happiest when we lose ourselves in some concentrated activity. Some people call that state "flow".[1]

There are myriad things that can make us happy—when we feel loved, valued or nurtured; when we achieve something; when we have a good laugh with friends; when we enter a space that makes us smile. Perhaps in a simple way we can say that happiness means feeling good, and enjoying life.

In the modern world happiness has been recognised as a worthwhile political goal—the US Declaration of Independence states that the pursuit of happiness is a fundamental right, in 1972 the King of Bhutan stated that his country should measure the Gross National Happiness Quotient as well as their GDP. Andrew Oswald, Professor of Economics at Warwick University and others suggest that a Gross Happiness Level may come to replace GDP as a measure of any nation's wellbeing.

In the eighteenth century a number of thinkers, including Jeremy Bentham, proposed that the aim of society should be to achieve the greatest happiness of the greatest number. This was interpreted by economists as "Happiness is the sum of good feelings minus bad; the pursuit of pleasure and the avoidance of pain." They even postulated a hedonimeter to measure the ups and downs of a man's feelings in the same way as a thermometer does.[2]

At the Royal Institute of British Architects (RIBA) there is a group called Building Futures which aims to promote discussion about the future of the built environment in, say, 20 to 50 years' time. We have noticed that, in the field of economics, it has been found that increasing our wealth does not necessarily make us happier. A new science, the Economics of Happiness, has sprung up and we have found that although GDP, which measures our economic prosperity, has increased enormously since the 1950s, our happiness has not.

The economists Bruno Frey and Aolis Stutzer have found that where there is a well developed democratic framework, coupled with a good degree of local democracy, people are more satisfied with their lives.[3]

It now also seems that we can accurately measure how happy we are. People who confess to feeling happy tend to grin more than others, and generally people can say quite accurately how they feel at a given moment, on a scale of, say, zero to ten. Researchers have found that people's self-reports tally pretty well with what electrodes planted on their scalp reveal about the frequency and voltage of electrical waves in their left forebrain, which is the area that lights up when they are feeling good. So some researchers claim that we can measure happiness quantitatively.[4]

What are the things that make us happy? A lot of what has been discovered is pretty much common sense:

· Those who are least happy are the divorced, and those in the lowest quarter of the income distribution.
· Women are more likely to be 'Very Happy', and also more likely to be 'Not too Happy'.
· Those who are unemployed are less likely to be 'Very Happy'.

I wanted to know whether architecture and the environment we build for ourselves can contribute to our happiness. Can it make us smile?

When I was asked by David Marks and Julia Barfield to collaborate with them on an idea they had for a competition for a landmark for the new millennium—the Millennium Wheel—their idea was to produce an observation wheel that would simply offer delight to those who chose to ride on it. Throughout the development of the design that we tendered, that was our primary concern. We wanted it to be an object of wonder. The fact that there are only tensioned cables that support the rim, and that the wheel is only supported from one side, means that you have to think hard about what makes it stand up. Modelled on the almost magical structure of the bicycle wheel, where all your weight is carried by steel spokes that are only three millimetre diameter, it looks almost transparent. Because the capsules are held on the outside of the rim using large cogwheels that are recessed into and hidden by the skin of their egglike form, you get no obstruction to your view. Great care was taken to choose optically excellent doubly curved glass, so that you can look down on the river Thames as it snakes its way through London and all of its landmarks.

Opposite Looking out from the Millennium Wheel.
Top Views from the capsule, unobstructed by
the structure.
Bottom Social interaction in a capsule.

My spirits lift whenever I go on it, and hear the softly murmured exclamations around me, and see the smiling faces.

Of course, architecture is about much more than providing a ride. And probably, just as the afterglow of a new pay rise soon fades, so such short term experiences are not enough. But I wondered if the way we design our towns and the specific buildings we inhabit could have a permanent effect on our psyche. Had anyone attempted to carry out systematic studies of how levels of depression were affected by aspects of their built environment?

At Building Futures we organised a seminar to which we invited people who had either been doing such research or who might be interested in that research. It became clear that there are many thinkers, researchers and practitioners who have been considering the topic. It could even be that developers and planners will start to consider happiness as a desirable objective, along with sustainability and social responsibility.

This book is a collection of essays by some of those people. It represents a wide range of opinions and approaches, and we hope that it may provide a stimulant for further debate, and perhaps more systematic research.

We start with the architect Keith Bradley who argues that it is the in-between spaces in our buildings that are needed for social interaction. The circulation spaces are not just a means of getting from A to B, with every extra spare square metre being seen as wasted money. He takes the example of schools, which foster communities and shows how these spaces can stimulate the interaction between pupils, and encourage feelings of belonging and happiness.

The architects Ros Diamond and Simon Henley also discuss issues of public space. Our streets and public spaces need life. But to be happy we also need to feel that we have control of our space and time. They remind us of the TV sitcom *The Good Life*, in which a couple convert their suburban garden' to self supporting agriculture, and the experiments of radical environmentalists and architects in New Mexico, in communities built on recycling and alternative energies. They also rail against the commercialisation of the public realm and those public buildings with deep section and expanded commercial facilities that are confused with the public ones.

Pooran Desai, Director of BioRegional Quintain who developed the BedZED housing estate, and the *One Planet Living Guide*, argues that happiness is the key to unlocking sustainability. On the estate cars are kept to the minimum and there is a car club. The layout encourages walking and meetings between neighbours. He builds on the theme that it isn't just the architectural planning, but the social structure that helps to bring about happiness.

Jeremy Till, Dean of Architecture at the University of Westminster and author, puts the brakes on all this optimism by arguing that we shouldn't be naively optimistic about our new architecture, and that we must take care to be realistic. He takes issue with the assertion that there is a direct link between architecture and good mood, and also with the association of beauty to happiness as an inviolate truth. In some ways he goes back to theme of the others, that the key task of the architect is to contribute to special relationships that enable good social links to develop.

David Halpern, who has been a policy advisor and now heads the Institute for Government, has been studying this subject

Queen's Walk and the new Royal Festival
Hall terrace, Southbank, London.

for some time. He describes an evidence-based approach to building happiness. He describes studies that measure levels of depression and those factors that improve wellbeing such as the positive effects of looking at greenery, as well as environmental stressors such as sound levels and the importance of knowing where the sounds come from. He tells of studies into student accommodation and the terrible effects that long, blank corridors can have on a student's psyche. Where the layout allows for a cluster of rooms around the shared facilities the students have much more predictable and controllable interactions, and are much happier. He argues that we should build on the growing literature and data sources and life-satisfaction and use the information when we plan our developments.

Professor Byron Mikellides, at Oxford Brookes' School of Architecture has carried out a thorough review of the studies into architectural psychology and the analysis of the human factors of design over the last 35 years. i.e. those studies that have been explicitly concerned with making better and more humane environments. He says that architectural education must include developing an understanding of the relationship between people and buildings, buildings and the environment, and the need to relate buildings and the space between them to human needs and scale.

Max Fordham, the renowned services engineer, takes a good look at the issue of human comfort. He asks if our demands for comfort are too greedy. We have managed to evolve as a species so successfully that we are in danger of overloading our environment and then going into decline or extinction. He takes as a given that it is through our senses that we experience our surroundings, and in particular he examines how we are affected by noise, light, temperature and smell.

He describes in very precise terms how our senses are affected by our surroundings, and how they in turn affect our mood or sense of wellbeing.

Dr Hilary Guite and Sarah Toy describe a serious action-research project being piloted in the London Borough of Greenwich. Dr Guite spent four years collecting baseline evidence on links between the physical and social environment. They are now moving to the to the implementation phase where small changes are being made to the housing estates, as a result of their research. They argue that subjective wellbeing combines with psychological and social wellbeing, and their research will show that aesthetics, form and function do have a relationship to mental wellbeing.

The environmental scientist, Lorna Walker reminds us that we need our built places to make us feel safe, and to foster friendship and communities.

The landscape artist Martha Schwartz believes that memory, associations, and connections all have a large part to play in how we feel about places. For example, the Grand Canyon can give you a great thrill, but for her the family garden will always win in her mind as a happy place.

The conversation that Ed Blake and I had with Richard Wentworth was based on a walk that he led in Camden. His conversation touched on many issues that contribute to how we feel about our cities. He talked about coincidence and recognition; about the pavement and shared space; of ownership of space; about the ubiquitous brick; of Modernism and old things and comfort; and the need for community. It was interesting to me that so many of these are recurring themes in the other essays.

Tamsie Thomson has written an essay that offers a review of work that philosophers, architects, researchers and sociologists have been doing for hundreds of years in an attempt to discover how the urban environment affects our psyche. She includes a bibliography that shows the breadth of thinking on this topic, and that should give us the stimulation to continue to take the subject of building happiness seriously.

Throughout the book we have included a number of short pieces by people who care about the built environment, who we asked to write about a work of architecture that makes them smile. The ways in which they have chosen to respond to our request demonstrate how elusive this discussion can be. But throughout the whole collection of essays and short pieces we find the recurring theme—we don't like places that make us feel alienated and out of control. The best places are those which let us feel we are control, and that allow for good social interaction and the opportunity to be at one with nature.

‖‖‖

NOTES

1 Csíkszentmihályi, Mihály, Flow: The Psychology of Optimal Experience, New York: Harper and Row, 1990.

2 Edgeworth, Francis, Mathematical Psychics: An Essay on the Application of Mathematics to the Moral Sciences, New York: Augustus M Kelly, 1881 (1961).

3 Frey, Bruno S and Alois Stutzer, Happiness and Economics: How the Economy and Institutions Affect Human Well-Being, Princeton Paperbacks, 2001.

4 Layard, Richard, Happiness Lessons from a New Science, Harmondsworth: Penguin Press, 2005.

HA-
HARCHITECTURE

LOUIS HELLMAN

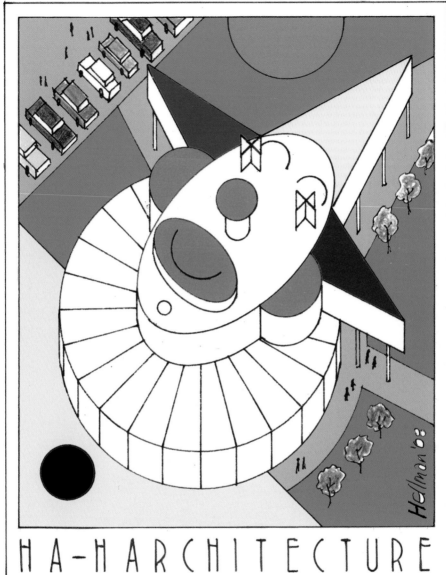

HA-HARCHITECTURE

THE HAPPINESS IN-BETWEEN

SCHOOLS SHOULD BE COPIES, IN
MINIATURE, OF THE WORLD AS
WE WOULD LOVE IT TO BE.
SANDERSON, 1892–1922

Happiness in architecture, in the words of the Danish
architect Utzon, is to "sense the mood of joy within our
surroundings". This is a personal as well as a collective
experience. Our buildings and spaces need to be vessels that
facilitate the basic human desire of social interaction—
places where we can meet and exchange thoughts and
feelings with each other. The relationship between people
and their places is the essence of life's experiences, often
happening at thresholds formed by entrances and movement
spaces; the 'circulation' places 'in-between'.

The true purpose of architecture is to help make human
existence meaningful; all of the functions such as the
satisfaction of mere physical needs can be achieved without
architecture. Without architecture buildings are reduced to
a schedule of rooms formatted in size, shape, and distribution
in accordance with their primary functional requirements.

The purpose for which the room is to be used, the activity, and how many people it needs to accommodate is described without identity and character. From the concert hall to the most modest of domestic living rooms, spaces are determined by what we now call a "programme" or "brief", although these are relatively modern terms. A whole industry has recently grown up around space-planning, setting out the requirements for every square millimetre of space. Most briefs for buildings, whatever their type, very rarely describe the linking spaces, the circulation, as much more than a percentage of the floor space (usually just above the bottom line of the area schedule which allocates a percentage for services and plant spaces!).

In modern space-planned buildings these 'in-between' spaces are treated as a pragmatic necessity, with a minimum amount of area in order to achieve a good 'net to gross' to satisfy the space accountants. This is nowhere more true than for educational buildings, and in particular schools. The 'guidelines' require the maximum amount of functional teaching space with the minimum of circulation required to serve it. The rooms get described by a detailed 'room schedule'—and the spaces in-between are left for minimum interpretation. However, it is these spaces that cause the most problems for children and staff. These are the spaces where 'unhappiness' often occurs. The lack of legibility, compounded by the 'assault' of noise, creates confusion, leading to anti-social behaviour. If the corridors, hallways, and lobbies are the streets and squares of our buildings, they are ill-defined, overcrowded, and abused. They are places that you rush through, spending the minimum amount of time, repelled by their utilitarian floors and artificial lighting.

Historically, circulation spaces have been given more importance. Spaces for movement, whether cloister, gallery or hallway, were planned for informal or ceremonial enjoyment. The routes from entrance to room, and from one space to another, had significance and value. The galleries of great houses were used for constitutional recreation, and the colonnades of colleges for interaction and debate. They provided a physical and symbolic transition from the outside world to the destination of private or public room; the threshold place of arrival and departure. The Greeks would conduct their politics in the stoas between the temple and the forums; a model for the local and central government gatherings in the 'lobbies' outside the 'chambers'. These spaces of movement and pause set up a social and physical structure of exchange, encouraging human interaction in allowing both rituals of routine behaviour, and space for serendipity. This balance of the known and the unknown, of predictability and the impromptu, are at the heart of our sociological response to our fellow people and places.

There is a current desire with certain promoters and sponsors of our new school academies to see these as a preparation for the modern commercial workplace, complete with the ubiquitous atrium. The corporate interior imposes a conformity of behaviour on the user, rather than stimulating a social and aesthetic response which encourages a relationship with the building and, more particularly, with one's fellow occupants.

Sociologists and anthropologists confirm what most of us feel—that humans are inherently social beings, and our happiness depends above all on the quality of our relationships with each other. How we interact with others is a crucial determinant of wellbeing; since people who care about others are probably on average happier than those who are solely preoccupied with themselves. The tribal behavioural patterns of recognition, belonging, and looking after one another are deep-rooted in our psyche. Jeremy Bentham, that great social reformer of the eighteenth century Enlightenment, said that the best society was one where the citizens are happiest. His early egalitarian views were to pave the way for a future Welfare State that would try to rectify the imbalance of rampant individualism and exploitation that is a counterpoint to the 'common good' that's rife in every generation.

The follow-on from an emphasis on the importance of relationships is the basic requirement for security and trust. Surveys reveal that the societies where this is most evident are the happiest—we need to feel safe and able to rely on the help and encouragement of others in our workplaces and neighbourhoods. This environment fosters relationships and friendships—a feeling of community. These positive, or negative, experiences form sensibilities early in life, and occur in our schools as the first truly communal building we experience after the relative isolation of the small family group that makes up home. Students learn how to foster friendships that nourish them and avoid those that are destructive. By this students learn to manage their minds, emotions, and bodies. Through this interaction there is self-realisation that leads to an understanding of what makes them distinctive.

Our schools' environments, and particularly the circulation and gathering spaces between classrooms, can stimulate these relations and a sense of society, belonging, and therefore happiness. Sanderson was the pioneering headmaster of Oundle School at another great time of social change in the early twentieth century. He said that

... SCHOOL BUILDINGS SHOULD BE BUILT MORE IN THE MANNER OF MUSEUMS, WITH LONG COMMODIOUS GALLERIES WITH WELL-LIT SIDE CHAPELS AS WORKROOMS. THERE WILL BE FEWER CLASSROOMS, FOR THE CLASSROOM IS COMPETITIVE AND DOMINANT REPRESENTING THE KNOWLEDGE OF THINGS THAT ARE, RATHER THAN THE SEARCH OF THINGS YET TO COME.

This education between spaces represented Sanderson's attitude to the breaking down of boundaries between rigidly-taught subjects. He believed in what would now be called a "holistic" approach to the curriculum, and if alive today would undoubtedly be at the forefront of progressive State Education. His philosophy was learning by doing, and he set up some of the first Science Laboratory Workshops in this country at Oundle. The practical art of experimenting and making were as important as the academic lessons; undertaken in 'open' workshop spaces freely available to the students at all times, creating an atmosphere of interaction and exchange. This created a more complete education, representative of an emerging second age of liberal optimism. He famously said that "Schools should be copies, in miniature, of the world as we would love it to be." His vision was of an idealised microcosm of life infusing a future society with values that are about relationships with others, the activity and the spaces that make up the environment.

Our practice has just completed a new building for Oundle for the Sciences, Technologies and Arts (called Oundle SciTec), working to the Sanderson principles of integration on the basis that it is at the interface where interesting things happen. The building provides the "commodious gallery" as described by Sanderson—a linking space, filled with light, between the disciplines for informal learning and socialising—places of movement between with views into the adjoining 'workrooms', and alcoves for pausing and gathering for exchange before and after classes.

During the same period as Sanderson, Rudolf Steiner the Austrian writer, philosopher, educationalist and architect

was saying that we should be "... making the whole building as if it possessed a soul". He believed that architecture should have a moral influence when it was experienced through "inward perception" and not just through "outward observation". The person who experienced harmony of form would learn to live in harmony. "Peace and harmony will pour into men's hearts through these forms. Such buildings will be Lawgivers...", (Steiner, 1926). Our practice has been working on the early designs of a new Steiner Academy near Hereford where these organic principles have been explored in relation to the changing requirements of the different age groupings. The classrooms have become 'houses' for the pupils and teachers; where they undertake most of their lessons, whether it be English, Science or Art, in a multi-functional single space. Specialist spaces for larger gatherings of performance, dance, music, exercise, etc., along with rooms that have particular equipment, take on the role of the 'public places' within this 'village'. The circulation, which is mostly protected semi-external, becomes the streets and pathways between the home classrooms (complete with front doors) and the communal spaces.

Opposite The Gallery and the gathering space.
Top The linking gallery, Oundle SciTec.
Bottom A typical laboratory, Oundle SciTec.

These 'cloisters' open out onto adjoining courtyards, which act as external teaching and break time play spaces—an interface with nature.

Post-war Europe saw the progression, in a more integrated way, of the link between sociological theory and architecture; the seeds of which were sown early in the century by people like Steiner and Heidegger. The 1951 Conference in the City of Darmstadt was entitled Man and Space, and attended by architects and sociologists. Hans Scharoun, 1893–1972, the German architect, presented a project for a "mixed primary school" (ages six to 14), which caused a sensation as a radical departure in school design. It was a design which broke the school down as a fragmented assembly of its constituent parts—an upper, middle, and lower school, linked by a meandering circulation space that opened out into assembly areas. Each of the 'schools' was designed differently in response to the 'growing consciousness' of the children as they progressed through the 'schools' and out into the community. The lower was the 'playing group'; the middle, the 'working group'; and the upper, the 'relationship

Left The courtyard, Northampton Academy.
Above Aerial views of the courtyard,
Northampton Academy.

of the individual to the community'. These parts linked by 'meeting cloisters', choreographed as an irregular undulating space that responded to movement patterns—this space also acted as a 'break-out' hallway for wet playtimes. This was social, organic architecture, with a disdain for imposed forms giving rise to an emphasis on open-minded discovery. Scharoun referred to a philosophy of 'place' as opposed to abstract 'space' and 'relationships' as opposed to 'objects'. The idea was of an extra spiritual / sociological dimension called *Geviert* (or "Forth-ness"), of buildings as sensual and not just visual experiences. Scharoun's subsequent schools adopted and extended these principles of humanist organic architecture with an emphasis on the spaces between.

At Northampton Academy we have followed this 'schools within a school' concept, with an organic linking of cluster classrooms around a courtyard. A cloister circulation route

links these groups, with an internal route at first floor, and an external one at ground level opening out into the central courtyard space. This space becomes the heart of the school, analogous to the city square, formed by a colonnaded edge of buildings. The courtyard, with its change of levels, is landscaped to provide 'districts' with benches semi-defining areas, which allow smaller groups of pupils to gather. The partially-covered edges provide more discreet places to meet or simply a more removed place to observe and partially participate when the mood takes. Children can find their place in the social structure of the large school community, and establish their own bases or favourite places to regularly meet friends—"I'll see you at our bench." The internal circulation at the upper level threads through the entrances to the classroom cluster 'houses', with their own double-height teaching hallways, linking the two floors with an animated staircase. This provides a focus for smaller groups of children and staff to identify a department of related disciplines. Each of these places takes a slightly different character through its detailed form, its position in the plan, and its use. The School Hall and Sports Hall buildings take the role of a town hall and church, as places to gather for events for the whole community, at the ends of the 'square' in this hillside educational settlement as a microcosm of the town.

This relationship of familiarity of typology, related to known places, with an emphasis on the spaces between allows a community to interact naturally in the way that we have been doing throughout the centuries. Design emphasis needs to again be given to these in-between spaces that provide the social network for the rooms of the brief or programme. Freed from the practical constraints of the room size, key dimensions, and environmental criteria required for the formal teaching spaces, the architect can shape these places of movement to respond to the nature of human interaction and the specific site requirements. To do this properly, within the modern constraints of the 'space budget', is extremely difficult. So we not only need to adjust the design emphasis, but that of the space and budget allocation to allow these areas to have the life they need. If a school where to be given a body analogy, the head being the hall and the classroom clusters the limbs, the circulation spaces would be the arteries,

Colonnaded edge, Northampton Academy.

with the heart as the principle gathering-space of hallway or courtyard. The connected life-blood of the place is key to the healthy and happy functioning of the parts as a whole.

The great American architect Louis Kahn divided architectural thought and design into the "known" and the "unknown". The known is the science of architecture, and our knowledge of the functional requirements of the spaces and the construction. The unknown is the ideals, dreams, aspirations, feelings, imagination, and intuition, as the threshold to the essence of the life of a place that is the true poetry of architecture. To do this involves the deeper understanding of what it is to be a fully-functioning and happy human being—an intense empathy with those who are going to use the building: their dreams and aspirations at a higher experiential level that facilitate a relationship with the place and the meeting of people. It is these heightened sensory relationships that evoke the familiarity and belonging that is surely at the heart of true happiness. Architecture can do this as a sociological art and at its best provide environments that are transformational. Architects must, like musicians, attain a greater understanding of the experiences of the art. This includes the principles of composition, of different realms of harmony and contrast, and when and why they should be used in the formation of indoor and outdoor rooms; the impact of light and shade, form and material, texture and tactility, lightness and weight, and of rhythms and how they lead to stimulation or tranquillity in the human soul; and the impact of sound and acoustics and how these can change an environment, along with the presence of people that affect the abstraction of space with their movement. These influences described by Erskine as responding to "the ballet of life"—both "comic and tragic" can in some way lead to a sense of fulfilment and happiness.

Opposite Cloister circulation route, Northampton Academy.
Above Classroom cluster, Northampton Academy.

THE
GOOD LIFE

ROS DIAMOND AND SIMON HENLEY

Urban life is characterised by our physical and metaphysical
experiences of cities, of how easy and pleasant they are to
negotiate, of their accessibility, and our expectations of their
use. Current cities are the results of political and economic
structures which have swung between state planned zoning
and free market development. They are usually a collage of
both; their appearance associated as much with their regions'
economic as their social strategy towards decline or growth.
Until the early twentieth century the public occupied the
shared external space between all building types, with urban
liveliness dependent on the mix of adjacent uses. In the mid-
twentieth century a different, flawed model was developed,
and increasingly used for regeneration, in which public
space was absorbed into massive amalgamated buildings
such as shopping malls and mixed-use centres. Here, public
leisure is controlled; corralled into amalgamated buildings
in which encounters are predictable, although circulation
is often duplicated. The legacy of new development should
be a more seamless and democratic city generating greater
public happiness. This is found in the recent alternative
architectural model, in which urban morphology and building
development are distinguished, improving upon the pleasures
of nineteenth century bourgeois urban life, in a typology
which is simplified into less complex buildings in terms of
mixed-use and public space.

Most large cities are having to address issues of physical
growth within confined geographical spaces, with land values
rising and a general strategy of building densification. This
development approach is being supported by a compelling

modern argument by economists and planners that urban life is the most sustainable, with its potentially reduced travel distances between places of home, work and leisure, and its efficient sharing of resources. However, recent urban densification has not necessarily produced more sustainable architectural solutions, but has at times led to a redundant and neglected public domain. Development which simply increases density plays into the hands of developers, appears to satisfy environmentalists and undoubtedly suits politicians. However, it often fails to generate new areas of public space.

The character of the city in its built form, is intimately connected to wealth generation, which particularly in Britain, is rooted in home ownership for the individual, and property development for private companies. It is an easy assumption to equate happiness to wealth, but the early twenty-first century city as a living environment, using a high density/low transportation model does not appear to be responding to what we might call "happiness generation". Levels of comfort and security described by property ownership are basic requirements: in the welfare led city, decent housing along with education and health facilities, were universal rights. Utilitarian basics were no more demonstrable as generators of happiness, than were the commercial private sector developer led versions. In his book, Richard Layard describes how for more than 50 years, citizens in Europe, North America and Japan have enjoyed considerable increases in personal wealth. However, in that same period there have been few signs that this has led to a happier population. Descriptions of happiness associated with our living modes relate to individual experience and collective enjoyments. In the city, they are associated with individual freedom; individual control of space and time. How often we randomly encounter friends on the street matters as much as how swiftly we can achieve daily tasks.

As well as the pooled and more efficient use of resources, urban life needs simultaneously to support the sociability of collective experience, without emasculating personal independence. Diminishing voting levels in British local elections, and the decline of direct action, reflect disbelief in individual influence. Its urbane expression is the safe public space which can be controlled by its physical securing. A dichotomy has arisen in our cities between the necessary spaces of circulation and those where we might socialise and linger, justified by the kind of building which has transferred public space to its interior, so that inhabitants are less

likely to use the street. The new urban territory found in the shopping mall and the urban skywalk in such cities as Minneapolis and Des Moines, has generated a duplicitous kind of circulation, draining life from the real street. Within it, a new kind of wilful late twentieth century mega-building type absorbs many uses under the same roof, controlling where users go, whilst proliferating excess circulation.[1] Yet definitions of happiness in the urban context relate to well inhabited public spaces. Urban sustainability requires what the urbanist Jane Jacobs described as the "staunchness of public uses"; the siting of public buildings to maintain or increase diversity, with mixes of uses which generate all day use and natural surveillance.

When issues of dwindling resources arose following the 1970s oil crisis, responses to consumption ranged from the 'back to the land' self-sufficiency satirised in the TV sitcom

INTRICATE MINGLINGS OF DIFFERENT
USES IN CITIES ARE NOT A FORM
OF CHAOS. ON THE CONTRARY, THEY
REPRESENT A COMPLEX AND HIGHLY
DEVELOPED FORM OF ORDER.[2]

The Good Life, in which a couple convert their suburban garden to self-supporting agriculture, and the experiments of radical environmentalists and architects in New Mexico, in communities built on recycling and alternative energies. Both ideas of sustainability were as much aspirational as they were technical. The presence of the allotment in the city was a way of making direct contact with food production, and the reintroduction of nature—as a way of taking individual control. In both cases, their objective was self-sufficiency and autonomy. This is problematic for a state economic model of Gross Domestic Product. Capitalism is not fuelled by self-sufficiency, but driven by profit inducing consumption. Its scenario requires the removal of the population from the land, from a more natural state, to place it in the space of the city, with its synthesis of entertainment and pleasure that Rem Koolhaas first described on the congested nineteenth century Coney Island, in his book *Delirious New York*.[3] One exceptional, contradictory example is the enforced pastoralisation of Cuba to produce food, and the 'allotmentisation' of Havana in the Organopónico project. This was a necessary initiative, which resulted from the demise of Cuba's sugar cane market and its guaranteed food subsidies with the collapse of the Soviet Union. The Cuban government created a self-sustaining food system based on thousands of "organoponicos", very small urban market gardens for growing food, in which the population, at first forced to grow food for survival, were introduced to the possibilities of the land within the city, growing and controlling their own food.[4]

In the speculatively dominated city, cultural and public buildings have become part of a programmed conception of collective leisure and happiness. Their architectural and spatial determinism merged into large developments. The multi-function public/private building could be categorised in two relatively recent models. The first is a result of indirect state subsidy from taxation revenue, used to fund public

Tom and Barbara Good, of *The Good Life*.

buildings such as libraries, concert halls and galleries, as a necessary component of the city. Resulting from publicly justifiable subsidy, it was economically and socially more sound, and it generated happiness in the occupation of the public realm.

The other model is the result of direct subsidy from planning gain derived from private development, invariably leading to ambiguous multiple function schemes, in which public facilities are amalgamated into private buildings. This is a bi-product of the inability of states to fund, and thus devolved political power. The outcome is the multiple use mega-building, a simplification of urban zoning which masquerades as mixed-use and largely determines social acitivity. It is a fundamentally flawed model for regeneration, symptomatic of a generation of buildings which seek to agglomerate internal and external uses. A system of planning gain implemented in Manhattan in the 1980s, in which public atria spaces were incorporated in the base of skyscrapers, in exchange for additional private upper floor areas, argued that it made more of the city publicly accessible.[5] The concession was subsequently cancelled because of the realisation that the atria spaces could be compromised by ambiguities about public/ private realms, and because they "added overbearing bulk to buildings in return for modest amenities". The densification of the city now hailed as sustainable, encourages mixed-use developments, in which public space becomes internalised and duplicated, with the generation of bypass circulation and its concomitant complexity.

In the past 30 years, an arts building type has emerged in which the container is the attraction in itself. The Centre Pompidou in Paris was one of the first, in democratising the cultural institution with the expressionism of its external services, and the escalator ride, originally offered as a free spectacular public view of the city. It has unwittingly led to the popularisation of a genre of bloated public buildings in which the architecture has become the attractor to the detriment of its contents. The large attractor, mixed function public building found its apotheosis in the deep section, internalised social and cultural centres of Rem Koolhaas and the Office for Metropolitan Architecture (OMA) projects, such as Zentrum fur Kunst und Medientechnologie, Karlsruhe, 1989–1992. These conflated deep section buildings usually contain expanded commercial facilities, which are confused with their public ones: in the case of the art museum, the cafe, and the gift shop, are somehow confused with the exhibits.

This amalgamated building type is what Mark Pimlott refers to as "the continuous interior", exemplified by the retail mall, a twentieth century phenomenon which has been applied variously, as an organising device, to education, healthcare, transport hubs and mixed-use schemes.[6] The result is the self-perpetuation of deep internalised public urban space which always needs to pay its way, to be rented, and managed. These schemes generate confusion between real public space, opportuning random encounter, messiness, exposure to the weather, implied good behaviour, and the collective space of retail/commercial/ cultural space in private developments, which are presented as streets, but are highly programmed, controlled, and predictive. Even private photography is controlled in the private environments of shopping developments such as Bluewater, with their own closed circuit surveillance and private armies of security guards, persuading users that these are safer and therefore better than 'natural' urban environments. This is programmed happiness; the loss of risk-taking, in which social transactions are no longer expected to occur in public space.

In 2005 Buschow Henley worked on a competition for the New Cross New Deal for Communities (NDC) to initiate the regeneration of a neighbourhood in the London Borough of Lewisham.[7] The brief for a one hectare site was to provide a new library, youth theatre, health centre, artist studios and affordable housing. Their alternative model involved a radical reinterpretation of urban happiness—public external open space as opposed to contrived public facilities. The NDC's remit was to devise a scheme in which the private sector was invited to redevelop a site using the capital receipts from housing development to subsidise the public buildings and community facilities. The brief required competitors to apportion sufficient market sale housing to subsidise the community facilities. The scheme proposed a quarter in which the buildings were more direct and honest in what they offered. It presented a challenge to a society which apparently places greater emphasis on wealth generation than happiness.[8] Buschow Henley sought to demonstrate how, in mitigating against over development, one could illustrate the emotional and physical value of land that is more normally lost through development, and its effect on individual and communal happiness.

Buschow Henley's strategy resisted the modern urban device of incorporating the public functions into a single monumental building. Instead, their scheme, which sought

Outdoor screening at the Meeting House Square,
Temple Bar, Dublin.

to identify how people like to collect in cities, configured individual buildings, such as a library, theatre, artists' studios, etc., around two new public spaces—a square and a 'Sanctuary Garden', the first vibrant, the second a retreat. This clarified access, reinstating it in the public external domain. It simultaneously reduced the over development generated by large areas of complex circulation associated with multiple use public (/private) buildings, where parallel circulation is created to access different functions directly, and circulate between them. The model used for the New Cross NDC project is efficient (net to gross), eliminating unnecessary and unaffordable space, which would otherwise need to be subsidised. The project highlights the dichotomy between the capacity of the city and its quality. Instead of congesting the city with oversized and grandiose public facilities, the design method reduces the proportion of public sector space, and the fivefold quantum of private sector stock, reducing densities and in turn freeing up land for additional public open space around which to plan these new facilities.[9] Buildings are designed with reciprocal outside spaces. They are not hermetic. The architectural element of the 'brim' Buschow Henley devised for Letchworth Town Hall, 2002, proposed in New Cross and subsequently employed on Goole's proposed Arts and Civic Centre, invites people to approach the building, to stand nearby, and to listen to activity within, as a gentle progression into the interior.

The 1990s development of the Temple Bar area in the middle of Dublin, used a modern version of the indirect public sponsorship system, where the scheme was initiated through a government development company (Temple Bar Properties). Temple Bar's combination of housing, shops, galleries, and cultural centres, was generated from a framework urban development plan won by Group 91 which was composed of eight architectural practices, to develop a very large redundant site.[10] The development eschews the megastructure of the plaza/mall or the single massive building containing many functions. It replaces this concept with a nineteenth century format, where the buildings each have one (or perhaps two) prime functions which are individually identifiable and approachable via their own entrances. In this case urban space is in a continuum with the rest of the city—its liveliness dependent on random encounters, and on the design of the street spaces, as much as the ability of the buildings to attract life. In Buschow Henley's model the attraction at New Cross that stimulates regeneration is not

THE GOOD LIFE

36-37

the possibility of wealth, but the availability of open space in which to meet and hold events, with the proximity of nature, in such shared interests as horticulture.

The principle of the technique of disaggregating use in buildings and creating archetypal external spaces, seeks to enrich and respond to the city's future collective use, generating experiences that could equate to happiness. In this way the city's characteristics arise from emotional and physiological experience, rather than from abstract and academic design principles. Just as time is considered a rare commodity, in the contemporary city space, the humanity and happiness it might engender is also a commodity. If the only means to regenerate neighbourhoods in a city such as London is to overdevelop, and the city cannot become more humane, then society needs to look for alternative versions of the 'sustainable community'. The over complex building masquerading as the richness of mixed-use has eroded diversity with artificially formed public spaces. The legacy of new public development should be greater happiness. It should target aspects of peoples' lives that our physical environment can influence, those which Layard states have the greatest impact on happiness: creating a strong sense of community, and placing personal health, nature and the environment at the heart of people's lives. Such diversity can be generated by development which accommodates accidental events and the random encounter, and in which the individual sentient being might experience delight and achieve happiness.

NOTES

1 See Banham, Rayner, *Megastructure —Urban Futures of the Recent Past*, London: Thames and Hudson, 1976. Two first formal definitions of megastructure: "... a large frame in which all the functions of the city were part of a city or housed. It has been made possible by present day technology. In a sense it is a man-made feature of the landscape...." Fumihiko Maki, *Investigations in Collective Form*, 1964.

2 Jacobs, Jane, *The Death and Life of Great American Cities*, London: Penguin/Cape, (1961) 1994.

3 Koolhaas, Rem, *Delirious New York: A retroactive Manifesto for Manhattan*, London: Academy Editions, 1978.

4 When the subsidised food system in Cuba collapsed in the early 1980s, average daily caloric intake fell from 2,600 to 1,000 to 1,500. The oganoponicos had to be organic because Cuba could not afford articial fertilisers and pesticides. See Viljoen, Andre and K Bohn, *Continuous Productive Urban Landscapes (CPULs) Designing Urban Agriculture for Sustainable Cities*, London: Architectural Press, 2005, Chapters 16 and 17.

5 A leading example is the IBM building , at 590 Madison Avenue between 56th and 57th Streets, 1983, architects, Edward Larrabee Barnes Associates, in which the atrium was designed in return for an additional 12,170 square metres of floor space. A Municipal Art Society report issued at a conference last month said that the IBM atrium, at 590 Madison Avenue between 56th and 57th Streets, "is universally lauded as the finest bonused indoor public space in New York City and most successful melding of social and aesthetic amenities ever produced by incentive zoning". Lambert, Bruce, "Neighbourhood report: midtown; Public Atria at the Heart of a Policy Debate", *New York Times*, 19 November 1995.

6 Pimlott, Mark, *Within and Without*, 2007).

7 Buschow Henley worked in conjunction with structural engineer Jane Wernick Associates, environmental engineer Max Fordham, landscape architect Jenny Coe and cost consultant Stockdale.

8 Layard, Richard.

9 The relationship between land value and construction cost, and construction cost and commercial value needs to be understood to refine the 1:5 ratio, a figure that will no doubt vary from site to site; the modern public commercial project assumes that a realistic profit margin on development is 20 per cent, and that all that income is to be invested in the public facility (which is unlikely), then excluding the value of the land, the developer needs to construct fives times more unnecessary stock to fund what the state requires.

10 Group 91 won the competition for the The Temple Bar Architectural Framework Plan, which was launched as an alternative to the commercial mega proposal for a new urban bus centre, planned by the Irish public transport corporation Coras Iompair Eireann (CIE) who previously owned the land. The practices of Group 91 were: Shay Cleary Architects, Grafton Architects, Paul Keogh Architects, McCullough Mulvin Architects, McGarry NiEanaigh Architects, O'Donnell + Tuomey Architects, Shane O'Toole Architects, Derek Tynan Architects. See Quinn, Patricia, ed., Temple Bar, *The Power of an Idea*, Gandon Editions, 1996. The completed scheme includes housing, mixed-use and the Arthouse, the National Film Archives, the National Photographic Archives, the Gallery of Photography and a Cultural Centre for Children, with the previously developed Irish Film Centre.

PAUL SMITH'S

HAPPY PLACE
CASA BARRAGAN
TACUBAYA, MEXICO CITY
1947–1948

I have always been a big fan of the architect Luis Barragan.
I love his simple lines, innovative thoughts and especially his
use of colours. As a clothes designer I am quite rare because
unlike many others that use lots of black, I also play with
colour. But colour has to be used in context at the right time
and in the correct place. Barragan does just that, his work
is mostly seen against bright blue sky and often in beautiful
open spaces.

One of my special moments and a place that made me feel
very happy was when my wife and I visited Casa Barragan
in Mexico City. Arriving outside I was convinced we were
in the wrong place. The street was very humble and some
of the buildings were quite run down and the exterior of his
house was very plain and colourless. On understanding his
work more, I realised the exterior had no colour because he
wanted to respect the neighbours and not impose his 'colours'
on the street.

On entering the house, happiness, life and optimism filled the
air. The pink interior with the sunlight streaming in, being
bounced off a perfectly placed gold leaf square painting on
a landing, onto the hall table. The adventure started there,
every new room and corner turned was special, exciting,
breathtaking and very inspirational. How ahead of his time
was he!

The entrance hall is always an important part of any of his
house designs; in this case it provides access to six rooms.
One of which is the living room, going from the enclosed

hallway you are confronted with an enormous window which opens out onto the garden bringing the outside in. In fact the land he bought to build the house has only partly been used and over half has been left for use as a garden.

I could go on and on for instance, the two dining rooms, one small and one large for eating quietly alone or with friends, the amazing stable door windows which create privacy but also provide light, the height of the rooms, the feeling of scale and much more.

The reason this house makes me happy is *everything about it*, but the main point is the atmosphere that is created through colour, light and scale.

Following pages Casa Barragan.

IS HAPPINESS THE KEY?
TO UNLOCKING SUSTAINABILITY:

POORAN DESAI, WITH ED BLAKE

Using happiness as a guiding principle can help us design our communities to increase their long-term viability. For example, we can design places with fewer cars, which will encourage walking, cycling and growing local food—all of which tends to make people healthier and happier.

The study of happiness is now a science. It transpires that happiness is a surprisingly measurable and reproducible metric. We can measure it, analyse what is likely to make us more or less happy, and use these findings to create happier people and places.

So what makes us happy? Things like good relationships, security in employment, our attitude to life and good health all make us measurably happier. People are happier if they are thankful and compassionate—and this can be cultivated through positive psychology. Activities like having sex and socialising also increase happiness.[1]

One major determinant of happiness is the levels of trust we have with our fellow human beings—and this has decreased markedly in countries like the UK as we have created more mobile and anonymous communities.[2] If we want happier communities we should foster lower levels of turnover, less mobility and places where people know their neighbours—places where people are less likely to become isolated. Isolation is a cause of mental ill health and can lead to people suffering from clinical depression and anxiety states.[3]

The petrol car is a major threat to the planet for the obvious reason that it burns fossil fuel and therefore releases large amounts of carbon dioxide into the atmosphere, which in turn leads to climate change. This seems like a cogent reason for minimising the use of cars, especially in our cities where their density is highest. There are other reasons why we need to reduce our dependence on cars. Cars have direct and indirect negative effects on our happiness. For example, cars might connect people who are far apart but at the same time they distance people from their immediate neighbours: there is clear evidence of how roads disrupt communities and local social networks.[4] A subtle process of atomisation happens when people drive alone. They can become disconnected from society. So the freedom of being an individual can actually reduce the chance for happiness. Instead we need networks which encourage us to see our neighbours face to face, get to know them, and build up trust. We can build happier

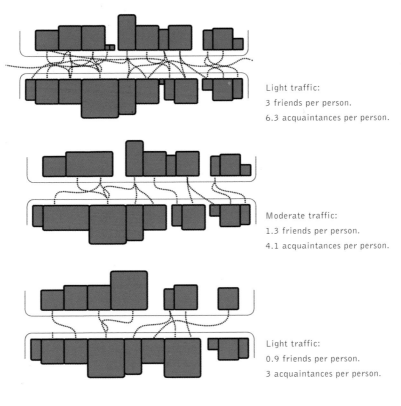

Light traffic:
3 friends per person.
6.3 acquaintances per person.

Moderate traffic:
1.3 friends per person.
4.1 acquaintances per person.

Light traffic:
0.9 friends per person.
3 acquaintances per person.

Statistics from Richard Rogers'
Cities for a Small Planet.

communities through better masterplans which are based on pedestrians and children friendly public spaces, where neighbours can meet and mingle.

One well-known pioneering example is the Beddington Zero (fossil) Energy Development (BedZED) eco-village in a south London suburb, where I live and work. Built by The Peabody Trust in partnership with BioRegional and designed with Bill Dunster Architects, its holistic design has promoted reduced car dependence—lowering car parking spaces from 160 to 100. This is achieved in part by having a masterplan, in which places of work are within walking distance of housing. BedZED is a mixed-use development with homes, offices and community space. BedZED residents who don't own a car can still access one when they need it—through a shared car club—but they are free to walk, cycle and use public transport for the majority of their journeys. Car-free public space has been created at the heart of the eco-village, a safe place which is enjoyed by children and neighbours. The community also has door-to-door vegetable delivery by bicycle.

Empirical evidence backs up the thesis that reducing car use increases happiness by improving community ties: a survey in summer 2007 showed that a BedZED resident on average knows 20 of their neighbours by name whilst the UK average is closer to three; and 70 per cent of residents report an improved quality of life over where they used to live.[5] Taking my recycling to the bins at the weekend often takes me an hour as I meet and find myself chatting to neighbours. As Jane Jacobs has written, "Sidewalk contacts are the small change from which a city's wealth of public life may grow."[6]

As Richard Layard states, "commuting is the single activity which people report as causing the greatest reduction of happiness."[7] Mixed-use communities enable people to live closer to work. With less time spent commuting, more time is freed for socialising and the family—activities which are enjoyable in themselves but also increase happiness through reinforcing community ties. Areas that are strictly zoned produce an opposite effect. Isolated dormitory suburbs and separate business districts create opportunities for crime,

Car free public space at BedZED.

with the former deserted during the day and the latter at night. By contrast mixed-use communities are naturally policed throughout the day, reducing crime—and, of course, levels of crime measurably affect happiness. For example, while the surrounding area is troubled by petty crime such as graffiti, BedZED itself has remained more or less graffiti free. If we are to believe Alice Coleman's proposition that social malaise can be measured indirectly by looking at markers such as vandalism and litter, then BedZED has little social malaise.[8]

Reducing car use benefits health as well—on a city-wide scale it will improve local air quality, improving respiratory health, particularly in children.[9] Not surprisingly, physical health and happiness are closely linked. Health improves happiness and happiness improves your health. This is supported with evidence that happier people live longer.[10]

However, we have built places and created lifestyles that do not promote health. Physician Robin Stott calls for a more balanced view of health.[11] We have focussed on treating diseases and: "have not invested sufficiently in the social and environmental factors that underpin true health".

Levels of obesity and diabetes are at epidemic levels with the World Health Organisation estimating that obesity is killing about 550,000 people per year in North America and western Europe.[12] In the UK in 2002, 22 per cent of boys and 28 per cent of girls aged two to 15 years were overweight or obese, predisposing them to diabetes, heart disease, low self-esteem and depression.[13] To see what the UK might look like in a few years, we might visit Florida, where it is common to see people so obese that they travel on electric buggies, unable to walk.

Professor Philip James, chair of the International Obesity Task Force, calls for towns and cities to be radically redesigned as planning public spaces around the car is one of the worst contributors to obesity. He highlights Oslo as a 'slim city' designed to encourage cycling and walking. Planners, architects and developers are the new frontline in health promotion.

As we have seen, there are a number of links between health, happiness and environmental sustainability. Most people have a clear understanding of what health is, and most people could at least tell you when they are happy, even if they find it hard to analyse and articulate.

The current preoccupation with sustainability came to the fore following the Brundtland Report which defined sustainable development as "development that meets the needs of the present without compromising the ability of future generations to meet their own needs".[14] It has also been defined more loosely as the integration of economic, social and environmental criteria, justifying almost every government policy or private company project. More recently, sustainability has been defined clearly through work on ecological footprinting by people such as Mathis Wackernagel.[15] Ecological Footprinting allows us to calculate how much of the planet's productive land and sea it takes to support a particular level of consumption.[16] Following this to its logical conclusion BioRegional developed the term "One Planet Living" to make sustainability more explicit and easy to understand.[17] Our understanding of sustainability is becoming far more precise.

Relating ecological footprint to happiness provides an interesting perspective. In the UK our ecological footprint has increased 70 per cent since 1960.[18] This increase in footprint has been accompanied by an approximate doubling in wealth, but we are no happier than in the 1950s.[19] If anything, we are slightly less happy. The USA and Costa Rica have similar levels of life satisfaction, but the USA has 4.5 times the ecological footprint of Costa Rica.[20] So enlarging our ecological footprint does not make us happier, and may if anything make us less happy.

Keeping up with the Joneses, fuels status anxiety, increases consumption, promotes environmental damage and reduces happiness. Once basic material needs have been met, happiness does not increase as we get richer, particularly if our neighbours and peers have even more than us. So for example, as Layard quotes, after unification, the standard of living went up in eastern Germany but levels of happiness decreased. Interestingly, it is not only the poor, but also the rich who are unhappier in less equitable communities.

So social equity, regardless of any moral stance, is a driver for building happier communities. Although social equity will have its origins in culture and politics, it can be expressed in good social housing and the avoidance of gated or economically segregated communities—something which the Danes and Swiss have been generally better at than the UK. This may be a contributing factor in the greater levels of happiness in their countries.[21]

Food contributes around one quarter of our ecological footprint.[22] It can therefore be a significant factor in the development of sustainable communities. As planners, architects or developers, we can consider how to facilitate more healthy and sustainable diets. On a regional scale, we have the opportunity to re-invent the relationship between urban areas and their rural hinterland to increase the availability of local, organic and seasonal food—so-called "bioregionalism".[23] We can also consider master planning to promote urban agriculture, farmers' markets and more allotment space, and consider community centres as drop off points for local food. Psychologist Professor Richard Stevens, as part of a televised experiment, *Making Slough Happy*, proposed a ten-point plan for happiness with his first recommendation being, "Plant something and nurture it." A second recommendation was, "Get physical—exercise for half an hour three times a week." So, to increase happiness and increase sustainability we should grow more of our own food. We could integrate herb boxes, sky gardens, community gardens, allotments, rooftop mini-allotments and edible landscaping into our architecture.

Can we really expect developers to tackle the wider lifestyle aspects that affect happiness? Is it their role? I would argue that if not them, then who? BioRegional Quintain Ltd, the property company, creates a "Health and Happiness" plan, which itself is part of the broader One Planet Living sustainability action plan for each of their developments. Schemes such as our Middlehaven project, based on a Will Alsop and Studio Egret West masterplan consciously brings together health, happiness and sustainability.

It might seem like social engineering to take a deliberate approach to creating places where we try systematically to reduce car dependence, increase the probability of knowing your neighbours, increase the amount of local food consumed, and try to influence the health and happiness of residents. However, social engineering is an inevitable consequence of what planners and developers do. We also engage in social engineering when we build roads, which inevitably destroy local social fabric and neighbourliness; or build out-of-town supermarkets which provide us with carbon intensive food; or create sprawling suburbs which force car dependence and promote obesity. That is not to say that we can guarantee or force people to be happy, but we can try to increase the likelihood of happiness being an outcome. What we design and build is so important to health and happiness in the long term that might we one day see Happiness Regulations sitting alongside Planning Regulations and Building Regulations? Perhaps not—but we can start applying its lessons anyway.

Increasing consumption is driving environmental destruction and is not making us any happier. Fortunately, science is now telling us that what makes us happy can also promote sustainability—indeed happiness can be a strategy for us to achieve sustainability. It might even be that promoting happiness will turn out to be the most important strategy to achieve sustainability—perhaps even more far-reaching than the calls to reduce carbon emissions.

NOTES

1 Dunn, E, Aknin, L and M Norton, *Science*, Vol. 319, 2008; Kahneman, D, Diener, E, Schwarz, N, *Well-being: The Foundations of Hedonic Psychology*, New York: Russell Sage Foundation, 1999.

2 Hall, World Values Survey, 1999.

3 Goldberg, David and Ian Goodyer, *The Origins and Course of Common Mental Disorders*, 2005.

4 Rogers, Richard, *Cities for a Small Planet*, London: Faber and Faber, 1997.

5 BioRegional, information to be published autumn 2008.

6 Jacobs, Jane, *The Death and Life of Great American Cities*, 1961.

7 Layard, Richard, *Happiness: Lessons from a New Science*, London: Penguin, 2005.

8 Coleman, Alice, *Utopia on trial: Vision and reality in planned housing*, London: Hilary Shipman, 1985.

9 National Air Quality Strategy, 1997.

10 Danner, D et al, "Positive emotions in early life and longevity", *Journal of Personality and Social Psychology*, 2001.

11 Stott, Robin, *The Ecology of Health*, Green Books for The Schumacher Society, 2000.

12 *The World Health Report 2002: Reducing Risks, Promoting Healthy Life*, World Health Organisation.

13 British Medical Association Board of Science, "Preventing Childhood Obesity", 2005.

14 Report of the Brundtland Commission, *Our Common Future*, UN World Commission on Environment and Development, Oxford University Press, 1987.

15 Wackernagel, M and W Rees, *Our Ecological Footprint*, The New Catalyst, 1986.

16 Global Footprint Network and Zoological Society of London, "Living Planet Report 2006", 2006. It tells us, for example, that as a global society we are consuming biological resources at a rate 25 per cent greater than the planet's ability to regenerate them; and if everyone on earth consumed as much as the average person in the UK we would need three planets to support us.

17 Desai, P and S Riddlestone, *BioRegional Solutions for Living on One Planet*, Green Books, Schumacher Briefing, 2003.

18 Global Footprint Network, *United Kingdom's Footprint 1961–2003*, 2008.

19 Gallup and World Values Surveys quoted in Layard's *Happiness*.

20 New Economics Foundation, *The Happy Planet Index*, 2006.

21 New Economics Foundation, *The European Happy Planet Index*, 2007.

22 Barrett, J and S Frey, "Our Health, Our Environment" paper for the International Footprint Conference, Cardiff, 2007.

23 Sale, Kirkpatrick, *Dwellers in the land*, University of Georgia Press, 2000.

RICHARD ROGERS'
HAPPY PLACE

*On 30 March 2008 Richard had a conversation with
Jane Wernick and Ed Blake in which they explored his
ideas about community and about how architecture can
facilitate happiness in our society. This is an edited version
of that conversation.*

Two things that are central to my concept of happiness are
culture and community. As an architect I would also say
that on the opposite side to happiness (i.e. unhappiness) lie
dereliction, alienation and brutality.

In our own office we had the concept to create a small
courtyard, which would encourage our sense of community,
and we deliberately created a place where people could feel
happy. The restaurant (the River Cafe) faces this square.

Being Italian, my happiness has a lot to do with food. In
fact Renzo Piano and I have talked about writing a book
called "Food, Sex and Architecture", which pretty much
encompasses everything that brings me happiness. Life is
about being happy.

You have a responsibility to stretch happiness beyond
yourself, and I think artists are the lucky ones because some
have the ability to do that.

The whole aim of the practice is to create a community—we
don't have ownership of our work, it is owned by a charity.
Each person who works in the office has a share in that
charity. After two years of working for the company (Rogers
Stirk Harbour) a portion of each person's wages goes to
a charity of their choice. So, we are also giving people an
opportunity to have control over there own lives through
our architecture. We also have a very good canteen. Having
control, choice, and good food leads to happiness.
In my own family happiness was directly associated with

food. When any one refused my mother's food it certainly made her unhappy. And I suppose that is something to do with joining in together, being part of a community. If a restaurant is done well then it can create an environment where community can flourish. Eating is something we should do together.

I am very much rooted in the idea that you should overlap the uses of space, because this allows exciting things to happen. In the space between the office and the restaurant people can come together and interact. We have a lot of birthdays in the square, in the restaurant and in the canteen....

The negative design for the sweat shop office that is ubiquitous these days is not conducive to happiness because it reduces interaction. We encourage people to go to the canteen not with their team but with other people. So they get to know more people, and extend the possibility of interaction and exchange of ideas.

The views and sight lines are very important to the space in the River Cafe. You enter the space and there is a 13 metre long stainless steel bar which is all about greeting. You follow an almost theatrical journey that ends with food and conversation, whilst at the same time you can see the River Thames, and children playing. I hope that it is the building that allows all this to happen.

Human relationships, culture, beauty are all aspects of my happiness, I some times see architecture as the umbrella that can contain all these.

Following pages The courtyard space at The River Cafe, London.

THE ROLE OF COMFORT
IN HAPPINESS

MAX FORDHAM

In order to relate happiness to my professional skill as an environmental engineer I am going to define it as "a state of mind which has developed through evolution to encourage us to behave in ways which ensure our survival".

Clearly this includes social behaviour, but here I am going to consider the issues that concern environmental engineers. The *Objectives of the Institution of Heating and Ventilation Engineers* states that they strive for the "greater comfort and happiness of mankind".

One of the problems that faces us is that we have managed to evolve as a species so successfully that we are now in danger of overloading our environment. This could well mean that we end up going into decline or extinction.

So, happiness needs to be refined in order that our demands on the environment for comfort are not so greedy. Over the last century requirements for environmental standards have become divorced from our subjective response to the physical sensations of the environment. For example, we set standards for an optimum temperature range that our offices should be kept at, whereas there could well be circumstances in which the design of those offices means that we would be equally, or perhaps be more comfortable at temperatures outside that range—e.g. if we can open our windows. We should return to an understanding of happiness and the joy that comes from feeling a wide range of natural conditions.

Fun outside in the cold weather.

We experience our surroundings through our senses. The feedback we get from our senses give us the information to confirm that we are vibrant and alive. Our sensory responses let us know if we are comfortable, and thus affect our happiness.

Any striving for happiness should avoid our bodies being subjected to stress. In some circumstances our ambitions can exceed our ability to be comfortable, in which case perhaps we should adopt a less ambitious lifestyle. For example, if we sleep when it is dark, and relax when it is very hot at mid-day we can reduce our demands on the environment. Whereas if we aspire to keep active for most of the time in those circumstances we will end up either too hot, or requiring more artificial cooling.

The ideas in this essay were inspired by the sort of research which is covered by Richard Layard's book, in which he describes how we can now accept that we can indeed measure levels of happiness.[1]

In this essay I would like to offer my thoughts on some of the key environmental conditions with which I concern myself in my professional life. These are:

SMELL
NOISE
LIGHT
TEMPERATURE.

SMELL
I will take it as a given that smells can affect how we feel about a place. Smells are often linked to particular memories, and so the smell of a wood fire, or even that of coal smoke gives me a warm nostalgic feeling. In a house the smell of cooking brings back feelings of support and succour. Shopping centres deliberately use baking smells to make us relax and therefore buy more. Of course, this would not necessarily make us happy. The whole idea of perfume is based on the idea that there are some smells which improve our feeling of wellbeing/happiness.

Smell is the most important parameter for defining how much ventilation is required for a building. The need to dilute smelly pollution by bringing in outside air demands more ventilation than would be needed just to provide oxygen for us to breathe. It also demands more ventilation than is required to clear the carbon dioxide we exhale.

The scientific approach concentrates on smell as a sign of pollution and has led to requirements for ventilation to control the odour. To date the relation of smell to happiness has not been a serious research topic. The current design approach is that smells are objectionable and a rate of ventilation is needed so that odour is not detectable. A person who comes into a room will immediately detect any smell, but after, say, quarter of an hour of being in the room they no longer detect it. A technique for measuring the amount of smell given off by people, processes, and building materials has been developed. This technique has started to be used, and has produced a notional ventilation requirement for buildings. A database of smell emissions is now needed so that the amount of ventilation can be judged in conjunction with the expected smell emission.

The current standards involve bringing in fresh air and then heating it to the room temperature, which consumes heat energy. Rather than restricting ventilation to save heat however, we can recover heat from the smelly outgoing air in order to preheat fresh incoming air.

In order to set proper standards for ventilation, the subjective sense of smell needs to be researched further so that we can better understand how much control is required.

NOISE

Noise, or sound, is important because it is one of our main means of communication. Many sounds, including music, can lead to an emotional response, and often one of happiness. Many people find music to be therapeutic to some degree.

When we design buildings we need to consider their acoustic properties. To do this we have to understand how the hearing mind works. The ear is very sensitive and can hear very quiet sounds from the sound of normal breathing at about 10dB up to sounds with 10 billion times more energy i.e. 100 dB-10^{10} (the maximum allowed in a public place). If we were conscious of all the sounds coming to the ear we would be in a complete tower of Babel and would be made very unhappy by the confusion. So the brain filters out the general field of confused noise, and we perceive only the loudest intermittent ones as sound. The background sound during a still night in an isolated country place is thousands of times more subdued than in a quiet suburban street at night. All the criteria for noise disturbance have to be adjusted to differentiate between night and day, and country or city.

Now that very loud sounds can easily be produced electronically with little effort, noise nuisance from neighbours is one of our common complaints. Currently the industrial approach to sound level requirements ignores the variable sensitivity. It is too restrictive in urban surroundings, and allows too much intrusion in the quiet country.

LIGHT

Light, like sound, also helps us to communicate with other people, and to experience our surroundings. Again, in order to design our spaces, we need to understand how the seeing mind works. We have evolved to be active mostly during the day. So, our ability to see in the dark is not so well developed as in some animals. The eye, like the ear, has a phenomenal range of sensitivity. The sun is 100 billion times brighter than the Pole Star and if we look straight at it our eyes will be damaged.[2] Also, the eye cannot encompass the full range of its sensitivity at the same time. It takes some moments to adapt to the general brightness of the field of vision.

A modern art gallery needs to have fairly low light levels so that the works of art are not damaged. A typical light level would be 50 lux. The eye can adapt to a halving of the light level in about three seconds. So, in going from a bright sunlit day (100,000 lux) the light halves 11 times which will take about 33 seconds. You need both distance and time to be able to go from bright sunlight to the sort of conditions of a conservation art gallery. Incidentally, these levels are about the same as our expectations for a traditional house.

We, who live in Northern Europe, are made happy by the warmth and brightness of a sunny day, just as we enjoy the feelings after having a feast, but this does not mean that we need to feast on this luxury all the time. Bright light helps the body to produce serotonin, which is thought to lift depression and aid happiness. On the other hand, people who are used to the strong bright sun associated with uncomfortably high temperatures seem to choose shady environments for preference.

Unfortunately, there does not seem to have been much research, and the whole issue of designing good natural

light to give a happy subjective experience seems to be in abeyance. We concentrate on brightness, but we don't have a consensus of opinion about the importance of the distribution of light and the impact of brightly coloured objects.

Modern technology has enabled us to make brightly lit interiors. So that the contrast between the interior of an office and the sky outside can almost be tolerated in the time it takes to turn away from our work and glance up at a bright window. In our modern buildings we have tended to specify bright lighting with the attendant use of carbon fuel. Does this really make us happy? Could we not instead design buildings with good natural light and provide effective shading do deal with the contrasting brightness that occurs on an overcast day when the sun suddenly comes out? Surely we can remember buildings that achieve this which make us happy.

Light and shade in a market in Marrakesh.

TEMPERATURE

I want to try to describe temperature conditions so that the feelings can be imagined rather than relying on the reading of an instrument.

As warm-blooded animals we have evolved to consume fuel and absorb oxygen to keep our muscles and brains working efficiently. We need to maintain a stable blood temperature. Otherwise we feel unwell. We have many involuntary mechanisms to maintain this constant temperature.

First, the flow of heat to the skin can be adjusted by controlling the capillary blood vessels near the skin. The skin is at a temperature somewhere between blood temperature and the temperature of the surroundings. If the skin is warm and the surroundings are cold we may loose too much heat. Then the blood flow to the skin is reduced so that the skin gets colder and we reduce the heat loss. If the surroundings are comfortable, the skin temperature feels alright. As the surroundings get colder we experience the skin as cold and feel uncomfortable.

If the air temperature is warm the body may have difficulty loosing heat and the blood supply to the skin is increased. The skin cannot get hotter than the blood so 37 degrees Celsius is the hottest possible. If the air temperature is higher than this the skin becomes wet so that heat is lost by evaporation. Some animals, e.g. camels can allow the body temperature to rise to 40s of degrees Celsius, but we need protection in such a climate.

The perception of comfortable conditions depends on the climate we live in. In hot climates people are likely to be happy with a fairly warm and possibly even moist skin. Those who live in cold climates expect the skin to feel dry and for the skin to be at about 35 degrees Celsius.

Secondly, recent research shows that people are more comfortable, and happy, when they can make adjustments in response to varying conditions.[3] We can adjust the heat lost from the skin by covering a chosen area of it with clothes. We can adjust the thickness and insulation value of the clothes. If the temperature is low and the blood to the skin is being restricted we may feel cold all over. We then put on more heavy clothes. The protected areas of skin then heat up. With warmer skin the heat loss reduces and the body begins to overheat. The blood supply is increased everywhere, including exposed areas like fingers which warm up and feel more comfortable. Exercise increases the amount of heat being produced, and needing to be rejected by the body. So it is a way to make us feel warmer and need fewer clothes. Just as we enjoy making physical movements as exercise for our muscles, so we can also experience pleasure by making adjustments for temperature. If our fingers feel cold we can get the body to increase the supply of warm blood to them by putting on a warm coat or even adding a jersey. When the conditions warm up we are pleased that hot weather has come at last and enjoy wearing light summer clothes. This is all explained by modern science. (See graph below.)

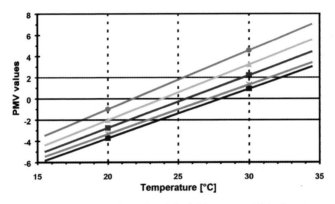

PMV values

Temperature [°C]

—●— Socks, shoes, briefs, long sleeved shirt, tie, light sweater, vest, jacket, heavy trousers

—▲— Socks, shoes, briefs, light long sleeved shirt, tie, jacket, light trousers

—■— Socks, shoes, briefs, light short sleeved shirt, light trousers

—✳— Flip flops, shorts, briefs, light short sleeved shirt

—■— No clothes at all!

This chart has been modified to show how people can adjust by changing their clothes. We need a social understanding so that people can be happy in winter with suitable fashionable clothes.[4]

The current engineering consensus, which has been reached by asking people whether they are "too hot" or "too cold", has arrived at a very narrow definition of a comfortable temperature. It does not allow for people making their own adjustments as small variations of temperature occur. This not only means that we use more carbon fuel, but also seems to lead to complaints by the occupants of the buildings, who feel they have no control.

To maintain a stable blood temperature we have to be able to reject as much heat as we generate internally. When we are standing in the strong sun we get a wonderful feeling of a warm skin, but the heat we are receiving also needs to be lost from our shady side. The radiation heat exchange is part of the happy experience.

Another mechanism for controlling our temperature is by means of air-flow over the skin. When the environment is generally comfortable, blood is directed to the skin and is close to blood temperature. Then a breeze removes heat, but the skin is being kept warm by the blood flow. If we are feeling a bit cold the blood to the skin is being a bit restricted. In that case a local breeze will remove heat and cause the skin to cool down. We experience that as a draft. Not a happy experience! If we are in a warm environment the blood is directed to the skin and tries to warm it up to blood temperature. We feel flushed and hot. Then a breeze, if it is strong enough, can be a cooling refreshing experience.

We need to calibrate what a breeze means. When I walk I hardly notice the air movement. That is about one metre per second and represents more than any trickle vent or mechanical ventilation system could produce. I bicycle at ten kilometres per hour, or three metres per second, which makes a real cooling feeling. It is nice in a hot summer, and it generates a need for warm clothes in winter. In a room, three metres per second is needed to be able to enjoy a hot summer day. To achieve this requires a really large open window area—at least one square metre of ventilation for one person.

Research carried out in Northern Europe tends to relate to people who expect their skin to be dry, so that the exchange of heat by evaporation of water/sweat is not considered important. Anyone who has compared the environment in Saudi Arabia with say Singapore realises how much difference the heat exchange by evaporation makes. I find it difficult, as a European, to imagine what either of these two hot climates are like. Normally, I know that I am not happy to be exposed outside on a cold winter day. But a combination of good clothes and vigorous exercise can be good at very low temperatures. I have certainly been very happy skiing at temperatures well below freezing. Coming out of the sea in a very hot climate is also a good feeling. And walking in the Empty Quarter of Saudi Arabia is quite likely to kill a European whereas a local Arab may survive.

It is possible to set up calculations to predict how people can survive in different environments, but it is much more difficult to know when people will be happy in those environments.

Modern research on thermal comfort certainly correlates comfort with climate so that people in warm climates expect a warmer environment than those used to cold weather.[5]

The point about this discussion is that we need to recalibrate temperature conditions in terms of happiness, because the modern consensus is that just using mechanical systems and energy to provide a standard set of conditions is not appropriate or sustainable.

INDUSTRIALISATION AND HAPPINESS
CONCLUSION

The Western industrial consensus is that increased wealth improves the human lot. In the environmental field wealth and energy enable us to remove the extremes of the environment in buildings, so that we are not forced to experience conditions that might represent a threat to our existence. However, we then aim to optimise the conditions to a very narrow range of parameters so that the amount of resources used is increased, and any chance for variety or contrast is lost.

The specification of environmental standards should be considered more in the light of happiness than in the interests of wealth producing productivity.

NOTES

1 Layard, Richard, Happiness, Harmondsworth: Penguin Books, 2007.

2 Rodieck, RW, The First Steps in Seeing, Sinaur Associates, 1998, p. 70.

3 Humphreys, Mike and Fergus Nichol, "Understanding the Apaptive Approach to Thermal Comfort", ASHRAE Transactions, Vol. 104, 1998, pp. 991–1004.

4 Fordham, Max, "Natural Ventilation", Renewable Energy, 19, 1999, pp. 17–37.

5 Humphries, "Understanding"

KIRSTY WARK'S
HAPPY PLACE

There are so many buildings that make me happy it was a
tall order to choose just one—and often I am captivated
by a chimney, or an elegant tall window or the shade of
sandstone, or the finish of concrete. I have settled on the
Burrell Museum in Pollok Park for a whole host of reasons,
not least the way it sits in the landscape. It is a building
which hasn't got what my friend Flora calls "a hit for
itself". It is modest and elegant, and function and form
are in perfect harmony, and it is an undeniably Scottish
building, with its huge facades of ashlared Locharbriggs red
sandstone. It is full of light which floods through glass walls
in the courtyard and allows a different view to the woods,
just metres beyond, every day. The Burrell Collection
finally opened in 1983 following a competition 12 years
earlier which was won by Barry Glasson, out of more than
200 entrants. He had to come up with a design for the
museum which could show off an ever-changing selection
of the 9,000 items left to the City of Glasgow in 1944 by
Sir William Burrell, a wealthy ship owner and voracious
collector (some might say plunderer!)—artefacts and
sculptures from ancient Egypt, Greece and Rome, Chinese
pottery, tapestries and carpets, three whole interiors from
Burrell's home, Chinese and Islamic art and so it goes on.

Barry Gasson said that it was to be an "a collection in
a park not a city...these thoughts suggested that the
building be placed alongside and close to trees... the
primary route of the building. It was a walk in the woods
and the woodland is linked to the tapestries at the centre
of the building."

As you approach the entrance to the museum you immediately know what joys lie ahead because you pass through the Hornby Portico, an eight metre high English Renaissance doorway which weighs 26 tons. Inside, the great Warwick vase greets you and there are treasures all around, ancient stone window frames set high in the walls, and beautiful stained glass panels set into the glass walls, throwing jewelled light onto an old oak bed with the Stuart coat of arms on the headboard.

I love the fact that Glasgow people have real ownership of the Burrell, and particularly at the weekend you can see kids racing around in and out of the rooms, enthralled by artefacts such as the lion headed goddess which I heard one little boy describe as "Darth Vader". In the summer families picnic in the parkland beside the fields of Highland cattle and drift in and out of the Collection where there is always something new to see... well something old really.

Following pages The Burrell Collection.

AN
EVIDENCE-BASED APPROACH TO
BUILDING
HAPPINESS

DAVID HALPERN

The built environment has big effects on subjective wellbeing
but, mostly, not for the reasons we think.

Here is the 30 second summary: We can empirically measure
whether people are happy or not fairly simply—although
there are different kinds of measures they broadly agree.
Many aspects of the environment, like levels of noise,
dwelling size or finishing details seem to have relatively small
effects on our long-term subjective wellbeing. In contrast, the
physical environment has a big impact on how we interact
with others—whether we experience other people as a
nuisance or a pleasure—and thereby on our wellbeing. A key
element of built environments that promote happiness is that
they lower the barriers to interaction, while also enabling us
to choose when, where, and with who that interaction will
occur. Get that right, then worry about aesthetics.

CAN WE USE EVIDENCE TO ESTABLISH THE IMPACT OF DESIGN ON WELLBEING?

Most people intuitively feel that the built environment
affects their subjective wellbeing. But there are several
methodological difficulties to establishing this with hard
evidence, although each difficulty can be addressed.

First, there is the question of what to use as a measure
of wellbeing. It is sometimes said "you can't measure
happiness"—but not by any psychologist who has studied the
issue.[1] The simplest way is to ask people: "generally speaking,
how happy would you say you are?" or "taking all things into

account, how satisfied are you with your life?" Answers are normally given on a scale such as from "not at all happy" to "very happy"; or on a numerical scale such as one to ten. People seem able to answer such questions rapidly and confidently, and their answers correlate highly with ratings of their happiness given by their friends and with ratings from independent observers. These simple questionnaire measures also correlate with more elaborate measures of wellbeing, such as 'day reconstruction' methods where people keep diaries of their activities detailing how they felt when they were doing them, or 'experience sampling' where a bleeper goes off and people respond with how they feel at that moment. Simple happiness and satisfaction questions have been used in surveys since the 1950s.

Another alternative is to study levels of unhappiness. These normally consist of scales asking questions about feelings of anxiety, depression or symptoms such as disrupted sleep, headaches or lack of energy. Such scales were first developed in the 1960s, and have been clinically validated against more detailed psychiatric judgements. In population surveys, such scales tend to be strongly and negatively correlated with simple measures of happiness: depressed and anxious people aren't happy people.

One can also try and deduce how happy people are through their actions. For example, if residents are not happy with where they live, they will probably try and move somewhere else. Hence one simple way of trying to get a handle on how people feel about an environment is to look at house prices. Of course, this method can get us into trouble if other kinds of factors are distorting prices or behaviour, so most experts—with the possible exception of economists—tend to be bit wary of using such 'expressed preferences' as a guide to wellbeing.

Secondly, there is a big problem of 'selection effects'. Suppose we find that there are a lot of unhappy people living in a run-down area in a city, whereas on the other side of the city there are lots of very happy people living in a shiny new tower block. Would we be right to conclude that the physical environment explained the differing levels in wellbeing? Of course not—or at least, not necessarily. The chances are that the people who live in the run-down estate are poorer and more disadvantaged on many more dimensions than those in the new building. Indeed, they have probably ended up living in the run-down estate, or have failed to move out, precisely because of these other factors: they have been 'selected' into the different environments. This type of methodological problem means that you either have to use very careful statistical controls or, better still, you need to study special circumstances where people are randomly assigned to different environments, such as in student accommodation (see the study by Baum and Valins below).

Thirdly, there is a problem of 'response bias'. If you're happy, the world looks good. If you're depressed, the world looks bad. So, if we ask a thousand people about how happy they are, and about whether they like their home or work environment, or the city they live in, we may find a strong association between being positive about the environment and wellbeing just because happy people are more positive about everything. This again demands very sophisticated statistical controls—such as measuring wellbeing before and after a change in the environment; or requires an independent measure of the environment by someone other than the respondent.

All these problems can be addressed, but they help explain why our bookshelves, and schools of architecture, are not filled with textbooks detailing the effects of the built environment on happiness.[2]

BEAUTY AND IRRITATION
There are a small number of studies that show that attractive aspects of the environment, notably such as looking out onto greenery, can improve mood. Patients who can see trees from their hospital windows have been reported to make faster recoveries and, more prosaically, people will pay significantly higher prices for otherwise equivalent houses that look onto green spaces.[3]

In contrast, there are a large number of studies that have looked at the negative impacts of various sorts of environmental irritations, or stresses, such as noise or road traffic. There is a strong association between complaints about the environment and unhappiness, but this is partly driven by response bias (see above). Tighter controlled studies find that in general, environmental stressors have a relatively small, though significant, impact on mental health.

A big factor that affects the impact of an environmental 'stressor' is how we interpret it—or what it means to us—

rather than its objective characteristics. For example, the impact of noise depends less on how loud the sound is than its content. Hence laboratory studies find that the sound of a passing car is considered far more annoying if it is thought to come from a teenager's hot-rod than if it was thought to come from a classic car.

In general, the evidence seems to be that we rapidly adapt to most aspects of our physical environment. What seems beautiful and attractive to a visitor rapidly fades into the background for the long-term resident. The classic illustration of this, in the wellbeing literature, is the finding that most Americans think that they would be happier if they lived in sunny California, with its perfect all-year round climate. Yet the evidence is that Californians aren't any happier—for their perfect climate rapidly fades into the background for the long-term resident.

My personal view is that at least some of the design details that architects and citizens seem to enjoy—let us call it beauty—probably do have an impact on subjective wellbeing, if only we took the trouble to measure it. So it is pretty frustrating how rarely architects or planners do measure this impact , especially since we know how to do it.

SHAPING HOW WE INTERACT

For most people, the greatest source of satisfaction in life—and the greatest irritation—is other people. A simple illustration is that the most important determinant of residential satisfaction in many studies turns out to be how you feel about your neighbours. This factor is generally much more important than what colour your walls are painted, how big your apartment or house is, or the style in which your dwelling is built.

Those who live close to you are uniquely well placed to watch over your house when you are away, lend you a cooking ingredient, or be playmates for your kids. Hence there is, unsurprisingly, a robust relationship between propinquity and friendship. But what is sometimes forgotten, is that your neighbours are also uniquely well-placed to make your life hell. In fact, there is a much stronger relationship between propinquity and people you hate, than between propinquity and friendship.[4] Whether you end up hating or loving your neighbours turns out to rest heavily on the design of the physical environment.

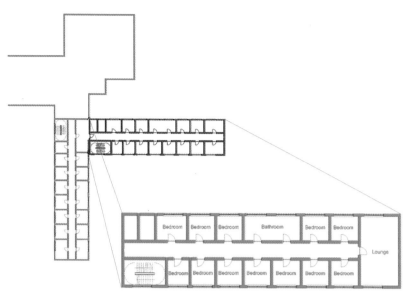

The effect of the built environment on how people interact has been clearly shown by studies of student accommodation. Such studies are particularly powerful because students are generally randomly allocated to their accommodation, at least in the first year, so researchers can be confident that the effects are from the environment, not some other factor.

In one particularly powerful study, the experiences and behaviours of students living in a classic 'double-loaded corridor' design were contrasted with those living in a 'suite' design. A corridor design is the standard format for college accommodation—15 to 20 bedrooms that all open onto a long corridor, with a block of bathroom facilities in the centre. In contrast, the suite design had clusters of three bedrooms, with a small lounge and toilet between them. This was a US study, so in both designs there also two or three students per room.

So what happened? Despite there being no initial differences between the student populations, those living on the corridor designs rapidly came to complain about the "excessive, unwanted, and uncontrollable interaction" with fellow students. Corridor design students exhibited more withdrawal; group formation in the corridor dormitories was inhibited; and the students were less likely to stay as room-mates in subsequent years. Moreover, the researchers found that the withdrawal and hostility of the corridor design residents generalised to other settings.

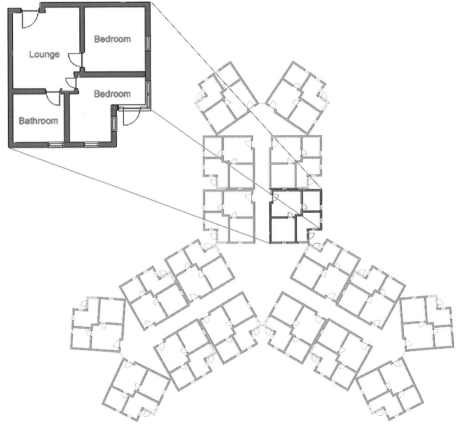

Lounge

Bedroom

Bedroom

Bathroom

Opposite and above Corridor and suite design
dormitories from Baum and Valins, 1977.

AN EVIDENCE-BASED APPROACH TO BUILDING HAPPINESS

Hence in a seemingly unrelated situation (a waiting room elsewhere on campus), corridor residents were found to sit further away from other people, avoid eye contact, and to initiate fewer conversations. Despite all this avoidance behaviour, the corridor residents still ended up feeling more stressed in the presence of a stranger (self-report data were subsequently gathered). In short, the students who lived on the corridor design found that the physical layout forced them into social interaction that they could not control, leaving them feeling stressed and hostile to other residents. So, they adopted a strategy of physical and psychological withdrawal that changed their behaviour not only in the dorm but outside it too.

An interesting aside is to note that, in design terms, the corridor design is very efficient. Bringing together the services (bathrooms) means that it is much more likely that when you need to use them there will be one available (in the suites, it is pretty likely that one of your room-mates will get there first). This is a design choice that often presents itself, and reinforces the logic of bringing blocks of lifts together, or servicing large numbers of flats from a single grand entrance.

The problem with the student corridors is not just that the students are forced into unwanted social situations, but also that the corridor space is long and narrow, and generally without windows or views out. There is no function to the corridor apart from travel. It is not designed for good social interaction. It makes you feel vulnerable because there is no escape other than your own door. On the other hand the BedZED experience tends to show that if you do have opportunities to get to meet your neighbours, you are going to be happier. Part of the success of the suite design is that you meet your neighbours in the lounge, or even better, in some self-catering halls, a small kitchen. The key point is the opportunity to interact without being forced.

Another powerful illustration from a 'real world' case is quoted in Newman, 1980, of where workmen put up a fence around one of the notorious Pruit-Igoe blocks in St Louis— people started occupying the outside space, in particular the previously abandoned benches at the front of the building, and the social atmosphere of the building was changed. Residents subsequently lobbied for the fence to be retained.

The moral of the student accommodation study, replicated in numerous real world housing projects, is that creating spaces within which residents are forced into unwanted, unpredictable and unavoidable social interactions—or even the possibility of such—with large numbers of other residents tends to lead to withdrawal, and not to positive social interaction. Classic examples are deck-access developments—the streets in the sky—that inadvertently created a maze of routes through estates. Instead of being places where neighbours would hang out and get to know each other, decks became places of fear and withdrawal.

Confirmation of these effects comes from design interventions that give residents back a sense of control over these overly public spaces. In the student accommodation, it was found that almost all the negative effects of the corridor design could be eliminated by the simple addition of a series of doors across the corridor thereby breaking it up into smaller lengths. So that when a student opened their own door they would not be confronted by the prospect of bumping into 40 or 50 possible other students.[5]

In one intervention—that I studied myself back in the 1990s—alleyways were closed to the public, and as is increasingly standard practice, keys were given to the residents on either side in one part of a Radburn layout housing estate that had become characterised by withdrawal, fear and high rates of depression.[6] This simple intervention meant that when someone opened their front door, if there was a person there, they were almost certain to be a near neighbour, rather than a relative stranger cutting through the estate as would have been the case before the intervention. Levels of social support—the perceived helpfulness and willingness of neighbours to help each other—rose dramatically over the year following. Levels of anxiety more than halved, and levels of depression—as measured by a clinically validated scale—fell by more than 80 per cent.

This structuring of social space helps to explain a wide variety of other effects of the built environment on wellbeing. For example, Willmott found in a study of Dagenham in the 1960s, that residents living on 'banjos' (cul-de-sacs) seemed to be happier than those living on through roads, a result that was subsequently replicated on large data-sets.[7] People living on smaller roads and cul-de-sacs can be far more confident that those they see outside their front doors are neighbours, and the lower level of traffic also makes it a more pleasant space to interact in. In contrast, various studies have found that residents in houses at the ends of streets, such that they face directly into a larger through-route, are much more likely to become social isolates.[8]

In short, the character of social relationships are powerfully affected by the extent to which the physical spaces around homes give residents the opportunity to interact with others, and also provide the ability to choose when and who to interact with.

PROCESS, SYMBOL AND AESTHETICS

An absolutely key variable for psychological wellbeing is control. In some sense, we have already seen this above in relation to controlling who we interact with, but it also applies to the physical environment itself. A simple empirical illustration—though open to a number of interpretations—is the higher life satisfaction of home-owners rather than renters. More dramatically, the impact of control—or the loss of control—on wellbeing is illustrated by studies of the threat of demolition. This sense of lack of control over your environment, even with the promise of being re-housed on site, has been shown to have powerful impacts on the mental and physical wellbeing of residents even if nothing actually happens.[9]

We might note that the wellbeing impacts of built environments also rest heavily on our aspirations and culturally specific view of what constitutes a desirable environment. Perhaps the best rehearsed example is whether living in a house is preferred to living in an apartment. Until recently, Anglo-Saxons have generally strongly favoured houses over apartments. Within the UK, there is evidence that, especially for women, we tend to be happier in houses. But it is possible that much of this effect reflects our culturally based ideal for living in houses. This is illustrated by one Canadian study that found that while women were less happy the higher they lived in an apartment block, men were more happy the higher they lived. The authors concluded that the main driver of the difference was the 'idealised image' that the residents had of their preferred dwelling, rather than any other 'objective' effect.

I have to confess, I nearly became an architect myself. One of the reasons why I did not was the results of an experiment I conducted while a final year natural scientist at Cambridge. This experiment involved showing a mixture of images of buildings and faces to student subjects who were either architects or 'normals' (i.e. Natural Science or other arts students) to see whether their liking for the building or face was affected by how often they saw it.[10] One side result was that, while architectural or other students agreed very highly on the attractiveness of faces, there was almost no relationship between their ratings of the attractiveness of buildings. This divergence between the preferences of 'normals' and architects got larger the longer the students had been studying architecture.

This amusing result has some pretty serious, and obvious, consequences. You could see why the relationship between architects and clients was not always going to be a happy one if their aesthetic ideals ended up so different from that of the likely end users of their buildings. This aesthetic divergence, together with the importance of control in wellbeing, emphasises the ongoing need for architects and designers to maintain an ongoing dialogue with the wider community.

CONCLUSION: GOOD FENCES MAKE GOOD NEIGHBOURS
In a large evaluation of the 'good neighbours' schemes of the 1970s, Bulmer concluded that the main lesson was that "good fences make good neighbours".[11] Broadly speaking, three decades of research have reinforced this conclusion. Physical spaces can create opportunities for people to interact with each other, but if they simply force large numbers into contact then residents adopt a strategy of withdrawal and avoidance—either physically or psychologically. Literally and metaphorically, 'good fences' give people the power to choose when and where to interact with others, and make it easy to do so when they want to.

The implications go wider than physical design. Virtual spaces also have some of the same potential to lower the barriers to contact while still leaving the individual with control over who and when they interact. In one carefully studied case, an e-discussion list that was created for residents in a new neighbourhood was linked to a three-fold increase in interaction between neighbours, including an increase in sitting out on porches and informal, non electronic interaction. Residents also took to the habit of printing out key discussions and fixing them up in public spaces for those who might not have email.[12] Low-tech approaches could also work, such as creating neighbourhood or street directories with resident's names, photos and interests.[13]

The physical environment's effect on the character of social interaction has big knock-on impacts on wellbeing, as well as on related phenomenon such as crime and fear; physical health; and local governance.[14]

This literature also throws up a very important and practical lesson for designers and policymakers. Much of the resources that we spend on upgrading the physical environment, such as the new bathrooms and kitchens that tend to take such a large slice of regeneration budgets, appear to have relatively little impact on resident satisfaction and happiness. In contrast, other relatively inexpensive aspects of the physical environment, such as around improved physical security and the ability to regulate social interaction, have very large effects. The evidence is that these life satisfaction impacts are often much larger than those indicated by differentials in house prices.[15]

A key challenge for the design community in the coming decade is to turn these fragmented empirical insights into a powerful body of knowledge that designers, builders and residents can draw on, by building on the growing literature and data sources on life-satisfaction and happiness. Medical experts have, for several years, been able to compare the impacts of their interventions using 'quality adjusted life years'. There is no reason why architects and planners should not be able hold a similar conversation, but in a metric of happiness or satisfaction—and a conversation based on fact, not just fad.

NOTES

1 Donovan and Halpern, *Life satisfaction: a review of the evidence and policy implications*, Prime Minister's Strategy Unit, 2003.

2 See Halpern, DS, Mental health and the built environment, for a more detailed discussion of some of these methodological issues, together with more detail on many of the studies reported in this chapter, 1995.

3 One recent study of houses in Wales found that houses overlooking a park attracted a premium of £14,500, Dolan and Metcalf, *Valuing non-market goods: a comparison of preference-based and experiences-based approaches*, forthcoming, 2008.

4 Ebbesen, Klos and Konecni, "Spatial ecology: its effects on the choice of friends and enemies", *Journal of Experimental Social Psychology*, 12, 1976, pp. 503–518.

5 Baum and Davies, 1980.

6 A Raburn layout is where the roads run around the back of the houses, while the fronts of the houses open onto green pedestrianised areas. This study is reported in detail in Chapter Seven of Halpern, 1995.

7 See reanalysis of SCPR dataset, originally gathered by Morton-Williams, in Chapter Two and Three of Halpern, 1995. There is some evidence that roads that are curved, instead of straight, can also provide some of these positive effects by virtue of creating a visual enclosure of a smaller number of dwellings than a long straight road.

8 An elegant example come from Festinger's post-war studies of married student villages, again with the benefit of random assignment but in this case to houses.

9 Halpern and Reid, "Effect of unexpected demolition announcement of health of residents", *British Medical Journal* 304, 1992, pp. 1229–1230.

10 Through the course of the experiment, subjects either saw a building or face once or five times (from different angles). Sure enough, the more they saw a building or face, the more they came to like it, even if they could not remember whether they had seen it before or not—i.e. the effect is not consciously mediated.

11 Bulmer, *Neighbours: the work of Philip Abrams*, Cambridge University Press, 1986. The phrase, of course, comes from the poem by Frost.

12 See Keith Hampton's work, who has conducted interesting studies on the effects of e-neighbourhoods in the USA and Canada.

13 Paul Resnick has been looking at the potential of neighbourhood directories, also in the USA.

14 Halpern, *Social Capital*, London: Polity Press, 2005

15 Dolan and Metcalf, "Valuing non-market goods: a comparison of preference-based and experiences-based approaches", 2008. This paper shows how a £10 million regeneration project that appears to have little impact on house-prices, does have a significant impact on life satisfaction. When this is monetarised—i.e. you work out how much you would have to increase people's earnings to have the same impact on life satisfaction—it proves cost effective. That said, it would have been even more cost effective if the money had been focused on a more limited range of physical changes where the impacts were largest.

HUGH PEARMAN'S

HAPPY PLACE
DRAX POWER STATION
YORKSHIRE

If we are ambivalent about wind farms, and worried about nuclear power, we are in near-total denial about power stations burning fossil fuels. This makes my choice of favourite building a little bit tricky. It happens to be Drax Power Station, and Drax generates a lot more than electricity, of course: it produces terrifying amounts of carbon dioxide.

Yet it is there, and it is glorious, 4,100 megawatt engineering and architecture. It is a throwback to a time of enormous confidence in the power of old-fashioned technology. Although first planned in 1965, in fact it was completed in two stages, 1974 and 1986, and two years later added a desulphurisation plant. All this makes it relatively clean and efficient by the standards of such places.

At its peak, Drax generated ten per cent of all the electricity in the UK, using local raw materials: the Selby coal field, an enormous resource which had a far shorter economic life than planned. Even today, with its fuel sourced on the world market, Drax accounts for seven per cent of all our electricity. It is co-firing increasing amounts of renewable biomass (target is ten per cent of all its fuel by the end of 2009, allegedly the carbon-saving equivalent of 500 wind turbines) but it is obviously pointless to try to justify the place on environmental grounds. I chose it because it is simply the most wonderful kinetic object in the landscape.

It sits close to the confluence of the M18 and M62. It commands the Plain of York, mother ship of a flotilla of smaller power stations marking the old coal seams. The view of it from the Wolds to the east is sublime. And it is distantly in view from the Humber Bridge, another engineering marvel. I'm lucky in that I have been inside Drax, even travelled in a clanking miners' lift to the top of its 259 metre chimney, taller than Canary Wharf. From up there you can see the curvature of the horizon, look down on the twin circles of steaming cooling towers—12 in all, each 107 metres high—and feel the slight vibration caused by hot gases pumping into the atmosphere from the three flues contained within the chimney.

If it ceased to function tomorrow, it would still be wonderful as an industrial ruin, but there is no doubt that it needs its attendant cloud of steam for the full effect. Its impact on the flat landscape was very carefully composed by the design team: engineers WS Atkins and partners, architect Jeff King of Clifford Tee and Gale, landscape architect Arnold E Weddle. If you look at their original design report, it is striking how very deliberate this was. Something heroic was called for, they knew this, and they duly delivered.

It is, essentially, the biggest static steam engine you can imagine. It powers Britain, it looks tremendous, and it cheers me up to see it in action. As guilty pleasures go, it is incomparable.

Following pages Drax Power Station.

THE
LOVE AFFAIR
BETWEEN
PSYCHOLOGY
AND ARCHITECTURE

BYRON MIKELLIDES

The aim of this paper is to critically evaluate the impact that research in Architectural Psychology, and human aspects of design has had in the teaching and practice of architecture, over the past 39 years. During this period there have been many international conferences, symposia, PhD's, and numerous books and articles written on the subject. What has been the major contribution of this research to our understanding of people—environment relationships from both the theoretical and practical perspectives? Has this understanding by implication increased happiness in the built environment and resulted in changes in legislation or directives by the appropriate professional bodies and institutions?

I would argue that this significant multidisciplinary body of knowledge has contributed to a change in attitudes within the architectural profession towards a more humane environment. This has been achieved over the past four decades by teaching students not only to appreciate the psychological and cultural aspects of design, but to consider the subject fundamental to their education. We know this because of annual feedback studies carried out over this period, as well as from many examples of students putting this knowledge in practice when they qualify.

Architectural psychology, environmental psychology, people/environment studies, human factors of design or psychostructural environics, call it what you may, has been concerned explicitly in making better, happier and more humane environments. These preoccupations have strong and varied undertones and appeal to the social and behavioural sciences including psychology, sociology, neurophysiology, geography, and anthropology. To what extent is the architect better informed now, and how well do we use this new knowledge?

This brief account reviews the knowledge and experience of teaching Architectural Psychology to architecture students since the subject was born in 1969 at the House of Black Dell in Dalandhui, Scotland, (Canter, 1974). There at least five questions which need to be addressed:

1 Have research, conferences, books and journals contributed to an increase in our knowledge?

2 Has this knowledge been communicated to designers of the built environment as witnessed through the practice of architecture?

3 Has there been a change in attitudes towards a more humane architecture, after putting this research knowledge into the educational curriculum?

4 Have professional groups and institutions including local authorities and professional organisations, such as the RIBA and the ARB, influenced legislation and directives on such issues as accessibility, disability, crime prevention, human rights and sustainable development?

5 Can you build up happiness as a result of this knowledge by revisiting the old concept of architectural determinism?

In 1969 there were very few books from mainstream psychology or sociology which designers found inspiring or relevant to the practice of their profession. Richard Gregory's *Eye and Brain*, 1966, was one such book based on experimental psychology. Michael Argyle's *The Psychology of Interpersonal Behaviour*, 1967, which considered psychological needs and motivation in social psychology was also important. Ervin Goffman's book *Behaviour in Public Places*, 1963, was another major contribution from Sociology. Since then there have been numerous books, scientific articles and conferences on the subject in Europe and the United States. The reader can get a glimpse of this outpouring of empirical research in the selected bibliography at the end of this article.

The development of the subject can be seen in the 21 conferences on architecture psychology, widened in 1988 to IAPS—an organisation established to promote research and communication of these concerns about people and environments in theory and practice (International Association of People/Environment Studies). Future historians will be able to assess objectively the contribution of this subject during the last 40 years within the different social sciences, as well as its impact on the design professions. At this early stage, one can only undertake a "content analysis" of its development as reflected in the publications and papers.

It is difficult to define precisely the inter-, multi-, trans-disciplinary nature of this subject. For example there was hope for the future in the first conference in Dalandhui, 1969, that for the first time psychologists and architect would start to talk to each other. This was followed by the emphasis on methodology, listening and taking notes at Kingston, 1970. At Lund, 1973, there was the much needed increase in communication between the participants in providing first hand information that architects could use directly in design. Other conferences looked at green architecture, ecological perspectives, evolving environmental ideals, new ways of life, values and design practices to help the designer to create healthier, happier and more sustainable environments.

Left Walter Segal with Jon Broome on the self-build site.
Above Exterior of Walter Segal's self-build housing scheme.

The verdict on the first question raised is that a considerable amount of new knowledge and research has been accumulated over the years. This knowledge includes a better understanding of human needs, perception, colour, POE (Post Occupancy Evaluation) participation and architectural aesthetics, and above all, looking at objective as opposed to subjective criteria. Instead of appealing to the philosophical methods of enquiry (authority, tenacity and intuition) the architect appeals to experimental psychology.

Has this knowledge been communicated to designers and students of architecture, is the second question which needs to be addressed.

When we look at the world of architecture, a considerable amount of this research has gone unnoticed. Some architects are sceptical about its value in design and, as a consequence, design awards are given primarily for imagination and originality at the expense of the users' health, happiness and wellbeing. In 1984, Niels Prak's book *Architects, the Noted and the Ignored* provides us with a useful analysis of the self-image and self-esteem of the professional as opposed to the user.

However, a number of architects are offering us hope for the future, because they combine both originality and aesthetics with an understanding and ability to cater for people's needs. In some of these cases, the architect put their clients needs at the top of their list of design priorities.

Ralph Erskine is one such architect. In the Pågens Bakery in Malmö, Sweden, he has considered that occupants' psychological needs, such as the balance between 'contact' and 'privacy', as well as 'identity' and 'personalisation', while remaining very much aware of the occupants' differences in terms of personality and values. He also considered the need to change the open-plan Office Landscape for various activities, both co-operative or competitive. His comment that "neither buildings nor furniture solve social or psychological problems, but hopefully they can help", shows that he has properly understood the concept of "architectural determinism"—i.e. he does not make extravagant claims, nor does he reject the role of the creative and caring architect in improving and facilitating more humane environments. The answer to question five, i.e. "Can you build up happiness as a result of this knowledge by revisiting the old concept of architectural determinism?" has been simply and eloquently answered by Erskine.

There are other architects who should be mentioned in this context who have contributed through their own idiosyncratic approaches to making healthier and happier places for people :

Christoph Schulten's sensitive participation projects in Aachen and Bavaria; Walter Segal's projects in Lewisham and Stutgart University self-build housing for students; Herman Hertzberger's attempt to get people involved with their surroundings, each other and themselves (see projects in Amsterdam, Delft, Apeldorn); Lucien Kroll's motto "no inhabitant participation, no plans" and the late Charles Moore's dictum that "buildings, if they are to succeed, must be able to receive a great deal of human energy and store it and even repay it with interest" are genuine, non-cosmetic attempts to consider, interpret and translate the concepts of human needs aesthetics, health and wellbeing. (All these projects are well documented in the literature (Mikellides, 1980) and show how successful the collaboration between the architect and the residents on all aspects of design and building has been. In Lewisham for example the residents, in order to show their appreciation, named the road after the name of the architect—Segal Close. In Germany Shulten is always welcomed by the residents' social events to see how the various spaces are working.

However encouraging these examples may be, by far the best way of communicating the new body of knowledge is through education. The opportunity to critically evaluate the validity of their work in teaching and studio projects is so unique that to ignore it is to perpetuate the view that architecture is only an art, rather than the process of articulating form which reflects human life and emotion.

I believe that by far the main contribution that psychology can make in architectural education happens in the first three years of the course. Once the groundwork has been laid down it does not matter what formal course in psychology or human factors the student pursues subsequently. At Oxford Brookes we have developed a course that ensures all the students of architecture have been instilled with a "psychological eye" and are better equipped to search for those aspects that they have not considered in their designs before. The criterion of success is not to be found in the practical rules of thumb that are acquired, but in the general awareness of the nature of science in relation to our aesthetic and social needs. A few students will pursue some of these ideas and objective methods of evaluation

further; others will concentrate on a more theoretical interest, and a tiny majority will apply for a higher degree in environmental psychology.

The majority of architecture students go on to practise their profession. It is in this group of architects that we are most interested. For example Mats Egelius' award winning participation projects in Sweden are well documented. When a student at Oxford, he attended the Lund Conference, did research on the subject, wrote articles in the architectural media, a book on Erskine and put this knowledge into his design influencing peoples' wellbeing and happiness; he even lives in an apartment in the same housing block he designed for people through active participation. By addressing basic human needs in the Swedish context, of contact, privacy, identity, personalization and aesthetics, Egelius created flexible internal spaces, encouraged personalisation through colour, decoration and objects in semi private spaces; provided several communal spaces to increase interaction, and child caring facilities for younger couples. The impact of Mats and other people like him is difficult to measure but crucial to this research in making a difference to peoples' lives.

Other examples include the work of Gus Grundt. Grundt won the European Sustainable City Award for Oslo in 2002 following the guidelines of the European Union, for greener, safer and healthier places to live and bring up your families. The work of Phil Bixby in the 1990s, enabled poor families and unemployed people in the North of England to build their own homes by extending his traditional architectural role. Bixby, who followed the work of Segal was equally surprised by the ingenuity and ability of ordinary people to physically build their own homes and learn from each other. Bixby arranged for other professionals to teach them about electricity, plumbing and other services and how to learn to help each other in "group dynamics" sessions. As far as design is concerned, he included sessions of active participation with scale models and plans, and slide shows to enable them to look critically at other projects. Chris Trickey has, for the past 20 years has been designing with people in the South of England; in his firm's latest project, the Police Headquarters in Herfordshire, he included in his design the latest research in colour and light psychology. For example, he looked at which of the three colour dimensions of hue, chromatic strength and lightness is important for different meanings. Which of the three dimensions is related to excitement and arousal; does the passage of time go faster

in different colours. Do some colours make a space appear bigger? Are there any differences between men and women as far as colour preferences are concerned? (Porter and Mikellides, 2008). Examples from non-Oxford graduates include Omretta Romice's ongoing successful participation experiments in Glasgow, and Roderick Lawrence's ongoing concern about environmental health and healthy cities in collaboration with the World Health Organization. So, in answer to the third question, this subject can change the attitudes of architects, and has done so where it was taught.

I held this belief in 1968 when I started teaching the subject at the Oxford School of Architecture, where architectural psychology is taught as an integral part of the architectural studies. Students like the subject now no less or more than they did then, but they see its relevance to architectural education.

Opposite A view to the garden of Walter Segal's self-build housing scheme.
Above Interior of Walter Segal's self-build housing scheme.

In the first year students are invited to consider their role and image in society; they look at theories of visual perception, colour and light psychology, colour notation (the Natural Colour System), SAD (Seasonal Affective Disorder), proxemics (how we use space), cross cultural studies, theories about space and place and experiencing architecture through the various senses. There is a live project on Natural and Urban Aesthetics with a field trip to Westonbirt Arboretum and Bath in search of rhyme and beauty in nature and built form. In year two students experience and test architecture by doing live projects with real clients. In collaboration with the local police force, students consider problem areas in Oxford and they link theory to practice. They also do POE studies and consider principles of universal design and accessibility for all. This involves linking with former students' practices. Students' work is exhibited and judged by local architects, planners, city councillors and politicians. In year three students look critically at the latest research on the subject.

Architectural psychology has not been just a fashionable topic like many other trendy theories. Architecture should not only cater to selfish interventions but also, and to a larger degree, to pragmatic, habitable and healthy buildings which may not win design awards but can provide the inhabitants with pleasure happiness and joy.

Unfortunately, despite the positive contribution that psychology could have in architectural education, there is little evidence that it is universally taught, let alone integrated within the architectural curriculum in the UK. Amber Beare (1993) found that only parts of the subject are covered— human factors, colour theory and space perception being the most popular topics. The only other survey of its kind was a comparison between Sweden and England on colour research in architectural education by Jan Janssens (Lund) and Byron Mikellides (Oxford). 448 students in five Swedish and British universities took part in testing the students' knowledge on colour psychology, colour systems, myths and beliefs about colour. Despite the respondents' positive attitudes towards colour research, their actual knowledge was very poor in both countries. We think these results are typical and represent the situation in other schools of architecture in both countries.

The architect who has had no training in psychology or human aspects of design will either dismiss such research as being of no practical use (because he/she fails to understand it), or may view it with unrealistic enthusiasm, and see it as panacea for the problems of modern society. This is aptly illustrated by the government's eagerness to apply Alice Coleman's ideas on solving crime and vandalism as an easy, short term solution. Crime and vandalism have a social, psychological and cross cultural dimension and involve other solutions such as changes in attitudes and education. In addition to defining clearly the private and public spaces, one needs to consider, surveillance, management, landscape, and active (rather than cosmetic) participation practices. Perhaps we should move some of the emphasis away from architectural psychology towards a psychological architecture. For example, studio projects can include the concepts of accessibility, fire behaviour, and housing guidelines such as Ingrid Gehls' psychological needs of identity, control, security, experience and pleasantness, and different concepts of participation.

It is one thing to know about psychological needs and another thing to isolate the relevant ones for a defined problem within a particular social or cultural context. *Knowing* about human needs is an important first step, *understanding* these needs a vital second, but expressing them through their *translation* in built form is a culminant third. It is at this stage that the creativity and aesthetic sensitivity of the architect becomes critical. The architect may need to be inspired by nature and art, or learn from experience what natural structures people find beautiful, or benefit from architectural precedent and Post Occupancy Evaluation studies. Then he or she may try to emulate these structures, not by naively mimicking natural objects but by being inspired by the "relations between the artificial elements exhibiting the felicitous rhymes of natural beauty".

The architect can look up Peter Stringer's psychological models of man or woman: The "organismic" model characterised by behaviourism, ergonomics and anthropometric approaches; the "role" model having a sociological flavour, executing learned and internalised roles, and in the "relational" model when a person is active and acting, influencing and influenced by the physical and social environment. The architect may then decide which model can contribute to the elusive concept of happiness.

Finally, in answer to the fourth question, there is no better time to consider the impact of this research on human needs and aesthetics, on the design professions. By far the best way is through education. The European Commission Directive, Article Three, prescribes that architects should be trained and educated, in addition to design and technical expertise in aesthetics and the human sciences. In fact, six out of the 11 requirements are about these aspects. Nor is it a coincidence that the RIBA strategic UK study, carried out by past President, Frank Duffy in the late 1990s, sees that the top priority for change perceived by staff and students in schools of architecture is "a greater focus on design from human/social needs". Different countries have been more successful than others. In the UK this knowledge is incorporated in both legislation and different types of Directives. For example, the Disability Discrimination Act 1995, the Crime Prevention Act 1997, the Human Rights Act 1998 and the various Sustainability Directives and Agenda 21 are further examples where research has influenced the education and practice of the design and planning professions.

There is no guarantee, of course, that just because students have knowledge of Architectural Psychology that they will design better buildings; but they will be in a better position to design with people in mind.

Charles Moore once wrote that when people visit a place and like it or feel some connection with it, they send postcards to their friends to indicate their pleasure. Over the years many of my students have told me of the pride they felt when designing with 'people in mind'. This is a difficult test to quantify and administer but it shows the profound influence that Architectural Psychology has had on their lives and approach to design. By scratching at the roots of the question of happiness, health and wellbeing in the built environment, what better way is there than educating future generations of architects of their wider role, and the contribution they can possibly make. After all this is what they aspire to do when they start in the first week their course in architecture.

REFERENCES

Argyle, M, *The Psychology of Interpersonal Relationships*, Harmondsworth: Pelican, 1997.

Canter, D, *Proceedings of the Dalandhui Conference*, 1970, Surrey: RIBA, 1974.

Cold, B, *Reflections on Aesthetics, Health, and Well-being*, Ethnoscape, Ashgate, 2001.

Coleman, A, *Utopia on Trial*, London: Hilary Shipman, 1989.

Erskine, R, in *Architecture for the people*, London: Studio Vista, 1980, p. 135.

Goffman, E, *Behaviour in Public Places*, London: Free Press, 1963.

Gregory, RL, *Eye and Brain*, London: World University Library, 1988.

Lifchez, R, *Rethinking Architecture*, Berkeley: University of California Press, 1987.

Mikellides, B, ed., *Architecture for People*. London: Studio Vista, 1980.

Porter, T and B Mikellides, *Colour for Architecture Revisited*, London: Taylor and Francis, 2008.

Prak, N, *Architects: The Noted and the Ignored*, New York: J Wiley, 1984.

Smith, PF, *The Dynamics of Delight. Architecture and Aesthetics*, London: Routledge, 2003.

Smith, P, *Architecture in a Climate of Change*, Oxford: Architectural Press, 2007.

THE LOVE AFFAIR BETWEEN PSYCHOLOGY AND ARCHITECTURE

WILL ALSOP'S
HAPPY PLACE

Happiness can often be confused with many other sensations, such as contentment, tranquillity or smugness, to cite but three. These however, are mere distractions compared with happiness. It can be hard to judge the presence of happiness in others, just as it can be hard to pinpoint it in one's own mind. However, there are typical symptoms of the emotion, which we can notice in others, such as a smile or laugh, creases in the corner of the eyes or indeed a large erection. These obvious examples sometimes lead to more ambivalent signs like tears of joy.

We are able to recognise happiness because it is not a consistent state of being, it merely punctuates our existence. The qualities of happiness are therefore not continuous, for if they were, we would not recognise it. Although there are some universal triggers that can make you happy, I expect these triggers are generally different for each of us.

I do not believe that there can ever be a single place that will always make you happy, but there are certain places that come close. I do feel happy, very often, at the life-boat house at Sheringham, North Norfolk, at either 7.30 am or 7.30 pm. I like sitting near this happy vernacular building in June, looking west and knowing that to the north there is nothing sitting between you and the North Pole. You are pitched onto a powerful line of longitude that is almost directly on the Meridian. When I'm riding this line my imagination reigns and connects this small part of the earth's surface to distant and exotic places. Perhaps it is the near absence of *built* environment, while still having the comfort of reminders of human inhabitation, that is so conducive to my happiness.

In the morning the sun rises over Holland and works its way westwards to this former focus of the medieval wool trade.

The Dutch, who have interacted with the area for centuries, came to Norfolk to discover a less crowded version of their own country. The evening sun sets over the coast all the way to Blakeney Point some 12 kilometres away. As the sun sets and the cod run down the east coast, the dimming of the day reveals a hurricane lamp belonging to a beach fisherman, burning every 50 metres all the way to the point. In the early morning, on a calm day, the flatness of the sea is disturbed by the gentle ripples of the lobster boats returning to the beach, to send their crustaceous catch to the tables of London restaurants.

Being alone by a quiet building that is so defined by its context, in a place that is so defined by time, direction and weather conditions gives the opportunity for contemplation, reflection and timelessness, all of which can be fragments of happiness. I think other people enjoy this place as well but I have never talked to them—there is no need.

Some of my buildings make people happy and I am often asked how I achieve this. I always reply that I am delighted, but I have no desire to know how I do it. I do not think that the happiness garnered from buildings can be accurately reproduced from person to person. There is certainly no formula.

The lifeboat house at Sheringham is a very honest place. This simple shed is all I need from the man-made environment to make me happy, for a while at least.

Following pages The Lifeboat House at Sheringham.

SOCIAL
AND PHYSICAL FACTORS FOR
BUILDING
HAPPINESS
SARAH TOY AND HILARY GUITE

INTRODUCTION

This essay describes an innovative action-research project being piloted in the London Borough of Greenwich. After four years of collecting baseline evidence on the links between the physical and social environment in a number of neighbourhoods and building new partnerships across professional boundaries, the project is now moving into the implementation phase. Its aim is to improve the mental wellbeing of residents of Greenwich estates by carrying out a range of relatively simple, low-cost physical and social interventions which can be achieved within existing local authority budgetary constraints. The resulting impact will be carefully measured to provide evidence that changing the local environment can have a positive effect on people's mental wellbeing.

HAPPINESS AND POSITIVE MENTAL WELLBEING

The nature of any proposal on how to promote happiness depends on how happiness is defined. There are two distinct philosophies: the hedonic which defines happiness in terms of pleasure, and the avoidance of pain giving a sense of subjective wellbeing (from an architectural point of view this would cover aesthetics) and the eudaimonic tradition which describes psychological and social wellbeing (in architectural terms covering form and function). Eudaimonic happiness was first put forward by Aristotle and equated happiness with living a good virtuous life in which you realise your true potential (one's daimon or true nature).[1] This is a life with meaning. These two approaches have been brought together by

Corey Keyes into a concept of positive mental wellbeing that combines subjective mental wellbeing with psychological and social wellbeing and distinguishes between states of positive mental wellbeing with or without evidence of mental illness. For research into the built environment and happiness this means that we are interested in aesthetics, form and function and their relationship to mental wellbeing (happiness in its broadest sense) with and without mental illness.[2]

POSITIVE MENTAL WELLBEING AND THE PHYSICAL AND SOCIAL ENVIRONMENT

The challenge that we have taken on in Greenwich is to literally build these components of happiness into the physical and social fabric of people's neighbourhoods. We have undertaken research to understand the key areas or domains which are likely to mediate between the physical environment and mental wellbeing and then carried out original research to determine which of these are the most important to people locally.[3] We conducted the research in nine estates that were all in areas of deprivation in our borough. The dwellings had all been in the ownership and management of the local authority either in the past or currently. There were no apriori reasons to believe that one estate would be happier than another. There were a few differences in the age of the residents, but there was a similar ethnic mix and similar levels of deprivation on all the estates. The key differences were in features of the built and social environment. We have used powerful statistical techniques (multiple logistic regression analysis) to ensure that our findings, as near as possible, reflect true associations between factors in the environment and mental wellbeing and were not confused or confounded by relationships between residents' personal and social characteristics, their environment and their mental wellbeing. Figure 1 shows how confounding works. A factor in the built environment that we think influences how people feel may also be associated with some characteristic of the person, such as their income or their gender. These factors, such as income or gender, may also influence how happy people feel and if not taken account of in the analysis will 'confound' our understanding of the primary thing we are interested in—the relationship between people's built environment and their mental wellbeing.

An example of confounding is that of age. It is well-known in psychological research that people in their 20s are less happy in general than people in their 50s. In Greenwich we also found that people in their early 20s were more likely to live in high-rise blocks and thus a simple analysis could conclude that high-rise living makes people unhappy. By using statistical techniques to adjust for this potential confounding we found that the height of someone's home was not a significant factor in mental wellbeing once we had adjusted for the age of the respondents and other potential confounding factors, such as material deprivation, gender, employment.

These statistical techniques therefore allow a much more sophisticated and rigorous understanding of the relationship between the built environment and social interaction and mental wellbeing and have led us to identify six areas or domains and 13 factors that we think are essential for promoting mental wellbeing. The research has shown that both physical and social factors are important. Figure 2 shows the key domains on which we will concentrate. Table 1 shows the key domains or areas of interest.

Individual factors are those which are experienced at a household level and relate to the interior living conditions of dwellings, whilst estate-wide factors are those relating to the external physical and social conditions that may affect all residents living on an estate.

From this research we have identified three areas that are often tackled on an "either-or" basis; we argue that the challenge is to address these in combination in order to bring about mental wellbeing benefits. The three challenges are to:

· Carry out simultaneous improvements to the physical and the social environment.
· Carry out simultaneous improvements across neighbourhoods and at an individual/household level.
· Get social and health and built environment professionals to work together.

In practice this means that mental wellbeing will only be improved through a cross-disciplinary programme which includes a wide range of social and physical and individual and estate-wide interventions.

Each of these three challenges is discussed below drawing on the context and learning from the Greenwich project and some other case studies.

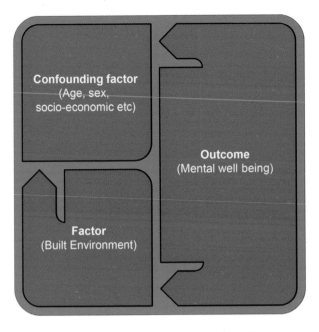

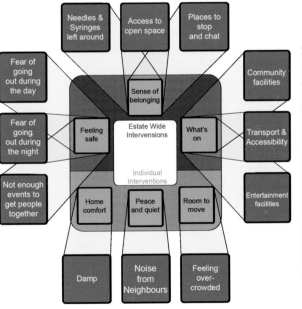

Top Figure 1: Confounding

Bottom Figure 2: Key domains (areas) that mediate between the built environment and mental wellbeing.

TABLE 1
FACTORS THAT WERE FOUND TO BE SIGNIFICANTLY ASSOCIATED WITH WORSE MENTAL WELLBEING

● ●

INDIVIDUAL FACTORS THAT WERE SIGNIFICANT

damp

noise

sense of overcrowding

ESTATE-WIDE FACTORS THAT WERE SIGNIFICANT

Feeling safe to go out in the day time

Feeling afraid to go out at night

Event to get people together

Places to stop and chat

Access to community facilities such as libraries

Access to green spaces

Needles and syringes left lying around

Access to entertainment facilities

Liking the look of the estate

Transport and accessibility[4]

● ●

SOCIAL AND PHYSICAL FACTORS

Each of the six domains in Figure 2 is associated with a number of statistically significant factors associated with it (Table 1). Neither the domains nor the factors can be separated out and all the issues are inter-related. The temptation may be to cherry pick interventions to get quick wins, but this fragmented approach runs the risk of having an overall negative impact. An example of this is that if new benches are installed in public spaces for people to sit and chat without improving the lighting, access or addressing social issues such as drug abuse or anti-social behaviour in tandem there may be resulting abuse of the space.

For example, where cars abut against people's downstairs windows removing the pavement and providing a barrier to chance social chats, this may be the result of a fear of crime. To address this fear, cars are parked close by in order to take prompt action in the case of burglary or vandalism. Community noise policies would need to be developed and enforced to ensure that those social chats did not occur late at night and disturb residents.

When we started to think about each of our factors we found that almost all require intervention on the physical and the social levels. For example, one of the most important factors linking the environment with people's mental wellbeing was having enough events to get people together. It would be possible within the built environment to promote this by ensuring that there are meeting halls or picnic facilities. But each of these require a social provision—someone to bring the meeting together, someone to organise the community picnic. The built environment is essential to promote these things. Support to, and empowerment of the residents to organise them is equally essential, particularly in areas where a high proportion of the population do not feel that they have the skills or potential to organise community events.

It is also interesting to note that some factors in the physical and social environment which may have been expected to have an impact on mental wellbeing were not found to be statistically significant in our study; for example, no link was found between recorded crime levels in an area and mental wellbeing. The important factor was people's perception of the level of threat within their environment which came from low level disturbance that would not be recorded in crime figures, such as groups of young people being noisy in the streets. These 'insignificant' factors are shown in Table 2 below.

TABLE 2
FACTORS THAT WERE NOT FOUND
TO BE SIGNIFICANTLY ASSOCIATED
WITH WORSE MENTAL WELLBEING

● ●

INDIVIDUAL FACTORS THAT WERE NOT SIGNIFICANT
height of building
house type—house, flat, maisonette
light, heat, draughts
year of build

ESTATE-WIDE FACTORS THAT WERE NOT SIGNIFICANT
density
recorded crime levels
sports and exercise facilities
shopping facilities
vandalism and maintenance
feeling that people can influence decisions

● ●

NEIGHBOURHOODS AND INDIVIDUALS

Our research has shown that many of the factors will need to be addressed through both an individual and a neighbourhood level intervention, since a focus on the individual's residence alone will not provide the wellbeing impact that would be possible without combining this with an estate-wide intervention. An example is that children were found to have impacts at an individual (household) level—e.g. contributing to a sense of overcrowding but also at an estate level—e.g. noisy or intimidating behaviour.

Figure 3, below, shows that there are systematic differences in levels of reported unhappiness on our estates. These differences are not explained statistically by the characteristics of the residents but are explained statistically by our 12 factors.

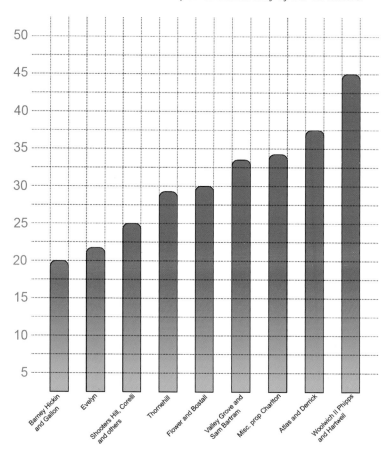

Figure 3: Variation in levels of reported sadness or depression over the last year by estate area.

One important estate-wide characteristic is "liking the look of the estate". There is considerable consensus amongst residents about what they do and don't like about their estates.

The value of improving neighbourhoods should not however detract from the importance of individual efforts to improve the environment. A garden, for example, provides a feature at the entrance to a block that is far more pleasant than rotting mattresses and supermarket trolleys that often litter front gardens in neighbourhoods with high levels of deprivation.

CROSS-CUTTING APPROACH

Mental wellbeing has tended to be neglected at a project intervention level because it is not the job of the planner, the developer, the engineer or the landscape architect and is not in any single person's remit within the local authority. In other words it has been nobody's responsibility. However, this has been changed with the new Local Government Act 2000 which provides local authorities with "a power of first resort" to "do anything" to promote the economic, social and environmental wellbeing of an area subject to the usual limitations.[5]

The project in Greenwich has found that, to address mental wellbeing in housing estates, we needed to share problem solving between different professions/sectors and residents. Existing channels and mechanisms can be used creatively to develop new relationships and shared visions and targets. The Local Area Agreement (LAA) is a useful vehicle for this and the findings of the new Place Survey will provide further incentive to improve the physical and social environment. In the Greenwich project we also involved Queen Mary College as an academic partner early to build the evidence base and to inform future phases.

MOVING FROM RESEARCH TO PRACTICE

Since July 2007 the project has been moving from research to practical action. This has involved identifying affordable and achievable physical and social interventions that can be delivered within existing council services. The main challenge has been to bring together a wide range of partners from the various departments including Youth, Adults and Older People, Housing, and Environment to understand the underlying principles and objectives of the project and to agree to work more closely together both with each other and with the academic research team.

To facilitate the process a Project Manager's 'toolkit' has been developed which defines all the possible interventions and the linkages/overlaps between them. To back up the toolkit, an "Intervention Manual" has been produced to showcase a range of different approaches through relevant case studies and examples from other local authorities. The idea is to inspire, enthuse and encourage project partners to think outside the box and be brave enough to innovate and do things differently.

The results of the intervention phase of this project will not be available until the end of 2009 at the earliest so there is still a long way to go. However, what the project has already achieved is remarkable in a small way: we have established a statistically significant range of factors that need to be tackled to improve wellbeing and assembled a diverse but passionate and committed project team from the public, private and academic sector to drive this project forward. The toolkit and manual have identified a wide range of practical measures that can be implemented to tackle these factors including:

· Providing fold-away desks, partitions and storage to reduce feelings of overcrowding in the home;
· "Prescribing" improved heating and ventilation to people vulnerable to respiratory infections and who have damp in their homes in partnership with GPs and the housing authority;
· Community cafes run for locals by locals with support from the local authority;
· Events and outdoor initiatives to get people together either to work on shared projects e.g. communal gardens or simply to socialise
· Seed planting in common areas.

Whilst the practical measures will be important the main gains will be from a new way of working across departments within the council and from partnerships in working with others who can promote positive changes in physical or social arenas.

CONCLUSION
Based on our research we are in no doubt that the built environment is associated with mental wellbeing. However, the relationship is a complex inter-linkage of social and physical factors and we need to carry out controlled research to measure levels of wellbeing before and afterwards to test whether interventions can make a difference. There is

no 'silver bullet', no one single approach that will address all the factors and thus improve wellbeing. So it is true to say you cannot build happiness in the conventional sense. But the first step is for professionals from all disciplines to acknowledge that where you live can have a big impact on mental wellbeing and, then, to develop a shared vision for how to improve the social and physical environment. We feel confident that a cross-cutting approach to promote mental wellbeing through the planning, design and on-going maintenance of an estate can make real, positive changes to people's levels of happiness. In a few years time we believe we will have the evidence to support this theory. We will know whether or not intervening on each of our factors will improve mental wellbeing. We will know what combination of interventions has most effect and if any interventions have unforeseen negative consequences. We will also know what approaches work and if there are gains in terms of residents' mental wellbeing from the cross-department working and cross-agency working that we are proposing. We will also know the costs of this and will be able to develop a programme to roll-out the most successful approaches and interventions across the borough.

NOTES

1 Ryan RM and EL Deci, "On happiness and human potentials: a review of research on hedonic and eudaimonic well-being", *Annual Review of Psychology*, 52, 2001, pp. 141–166.

2 Keyes CL, "Mental illness and/or mental health? Investigating axioms of the complete state model of health", *Journal of Consulting and Clinical Psychology*, 73, 3, 2005, pp. 539–548. This article describes mental wellbeing and mental ill-health as operating independently on different axes.

3 Chu, A, Thorne, A and H Guite, "The impact on mental well-being of the urban and physical environment: an assessment of the evidence",

Journal of Mental Health Promotion, 3, 2, 2004, pp. 17–32; Guite, HF, Clark, C and G Ackrill, "The Impact of the physical and urban environment on mental well-being", *Public Health*, 120, 2006, pp. 1117–1126.

4 Transport and accessibility were not included as potential factors in our original research as at the time there was little empirical data to show a direct link with mental wellbeing. Since then some research has been published suggesting a link and intuitively it seems to be strong candidate factor for improving mental wellbeing. We have therefore included this factor in our subsequent work though have not shown it to be statistically significant as we have for our other factors.

5 4PS Guidance 2003. Local government powers.

ANTONY GORMLEY'S
HAPPY PLACE

I can think of no better building to discuss than the one I am sitting in now, 15–23 Vale Royal, London, N7, the studio that David Chipperfield built for us four and a half years ago. When I say us, I mean it is for myself, my wife and the studio team, presently numbering about 12 individuals. At that time we were working from a small studio in South London, in Peckham, and the happiness produced as a result of the move is extraordinary. David has provided us with a building that is spacious, light, solid and lifts the heart every time we arrive. There is a wonderful feeling as you come in the main gate, the site is surrounded by industrial buildings that are densely packed and the experience of our front yard: a space of uncluttered openness is wonderful. The building works, and that is why it makes me happy. The building itself is completely free standing, it does not touch any of the party walls around it, and within it every space is independent, with its own direct access to outside. There are no corridors. There are two staircases that animate the facade. Anyone turning left up the staircase is going to one of the two private studios, a drawing studio for me and a painting studio for my wife. Anyone turning right is going to the office. There is a sense of purposefulness in the invitation of the building that is immediate. You go in through the big doors and you are into the main studio, a two-storey high room. All of the spaces are lit by natural top light.

The typology of the building, as David acknowledges, is a factory, but of a factory put to creative use. We have no problems (as we had had every day in Peckham) of variable levels, and the difficulty of putting heavy objects down in

any one place, straight from a 12 metre articulated lorry—
everything works, and it allows for freedom of action that
I have never known before. That combined with the fact
that we have a big open kitchen and a balcony that projects
about five metres square, where we have our lunches in the
summer, and the yard in which we can play football and
table tennis and skate. It is a great place to work, and has
also proved to be a great place for parties. I think that
everyone who works here has had their life enhanced by
the building.

Following pages Antony Gormley's studio.

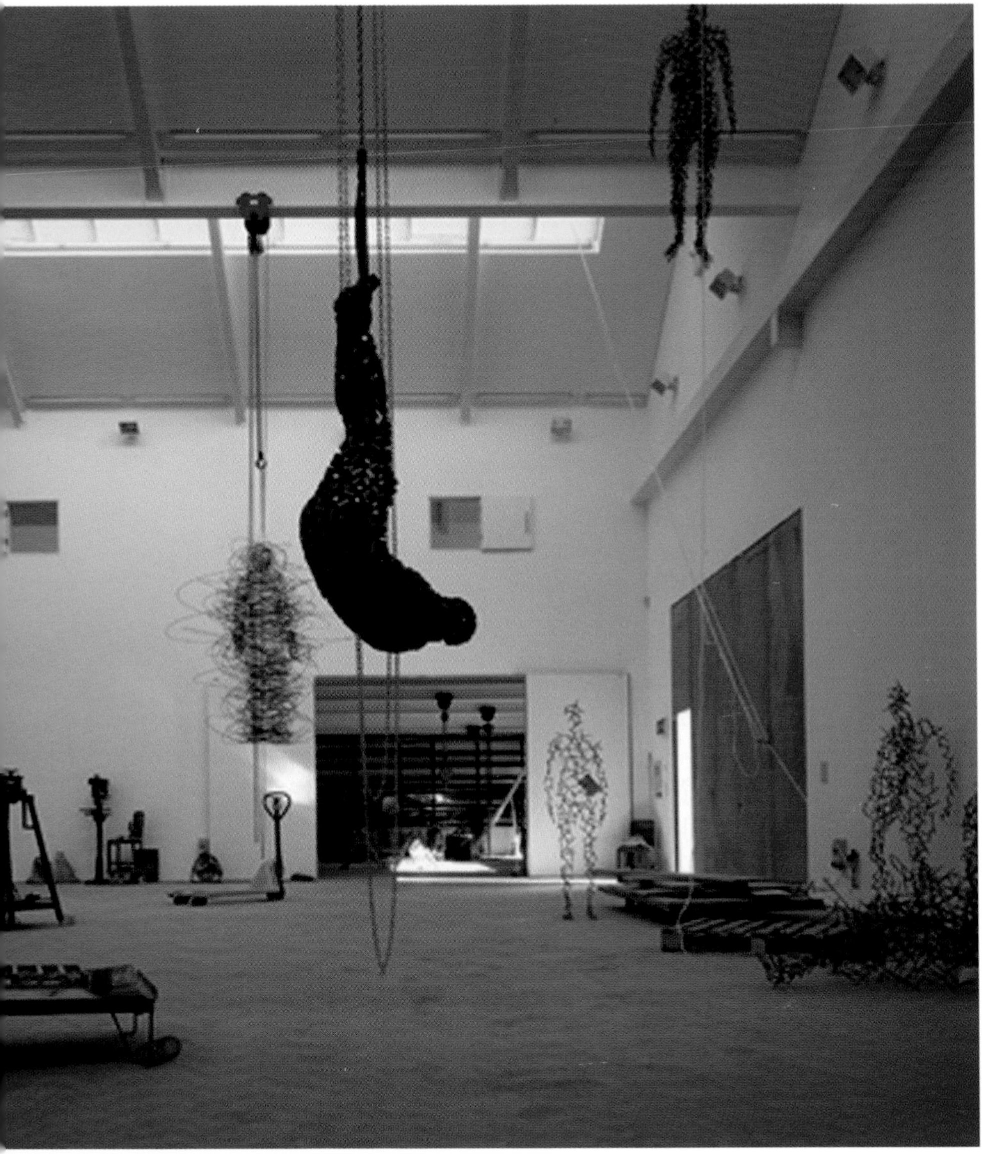

BUILDING FOR
CLOUD 9

LORNA WALKER

Few people would imagine a car park or a busy street as a 'happy place', yet this is almost exactly what we have been catering for when designing the built environment in recent years. By re-focusing on the needs and desires of real people, we can move beyond the simple provision of buildings, and the needs of the car and high street, to creating vibrant, happy and healthy places for human beings.

Evidence increasingly shows that our built environment is having a detrimental effect on our children, who are often left with nowhere to play and rely on, mostly, private transport to get them to and from school; on our health, with increasing incidences of heart disease, mental illness and obesity; and on our old and infirm, who have come to feel marginalised.

It is not the first time that planners and architects have been confronted with problems in the built environment. Planning itself emerged from a situation in our cities which Tristram Hunt describes as: "From the mounds of human excrement in the street to the dissolute gin palaces, from the smog-inducing factories to the dark and dank lodging houses, Britain's industrialising cities were a scene of unmitigated horror."[1]

At the turn of the twentieth century, and in the period after the Second World War, planning was concerned with countering infection and poor health, and providing residents and communities with basic securities such as food, and access to water and sanitation and housing. To this end, there was a focus on the provision of quality housing, allotments and green space, and infrastructure. Due partly to this effort, life expectancies and basic securities have improved drastically during the course of the last century.

Contemporary concerns are less obvious to the eye, but no less demanding. Climate change, health, crime and terrorism provide a confusing array of issues for consideration, but one thing is clear: the role of the built environment professional is no longer simply to provide basic securities. In the words of the government, it is to "create places where people want to live and work, now and in the future. They meet the diverse needs of existing and future residents, are sensitive to their environment, and contribute to a high quality of life."[2]

To define a rigorous and static framework for delivery is likely to result in blandness, almost the exact opposite of what we are trying to achieve. That said, "If you don't know where you are going, any road will get you there", to quote Lewis Carroll: we need some way of understanding what it is we are trying to achieve, and most importantly to secure the foundations for creating happy places. A good starting point is the United Nations Universal Declaration of Human Rights and the Declaration of the Rights of the Child.[3] The former declares that everyone has the right to a standard of living adequate for health and wellbeing, that everyone has the right to education, and that everyone has the right to participate freely in cultural life. Health centres, schools, libraries and universities, open and green spaces, and places to congregate can all contribute to achieving these aims.

Considering our children, those who will create the future of our society: how can we create places that give children the "opportunities and facilities to develop physically, mentally, morally, spiritually and socially"?[4] Reducing our reliance on the automobile and ensuring they have places to play and interact would be a very good start!

Another useful approach to the wants and desires of people is Abraham Maslow's framework, the "Hierarchy of Needs".[5] The hierarchy, also known as the Maslow Triangle, is often shown as a pyramid, with the needs from bottom to top being: physiological needs, safety needs, love/belonging needs, esteem needs and self-actualisation needs.

Following pages Children cartwheeling.

In the last century we have managed to provide for needs at the physiological and safety level, yet we must not forget the importance of them since they are the foundations upon which we build to achieve the needs higher up in the hierarchy: social needs such as those provided by friendship and family, and esteem and self-actualisation needs such as spontaneity and innovation. Maslow's hierarchy can in this way be seen as building on our universal rights, and showing us a pathway to happiness. From this we can begin to see how important the built environment professions are to delivering not only people's rights, but also their needs.

Besides the creation of whole new communities, one way of achieving this is 'incisions', or strategic investments to make some small improvements that can have a dramatic effect. This may be as simple as the removal of some graffiti, which has been shown to affect the occurrence of depression; the provision of some accessibility features; or, like Bellenden in south London it might involve hiring some local artists to brighten the area up with some unique designs.[6]

There is a richness and diversity in our population that we can work with to improve all our futures. Old and young, and men and women from all over the world inhabit our towns and cities, and they should be at the centre of our thinking. Our built environment should be beautiful and stimulate all the senses, which in turn will encourage creativity, innovation and art. We must have access to nature, to blue and green spaces that will keep both our bodies and our minds healthy and happy.

Creating a happy environment is about more than bricks and mortar, it is about our communities and our lifestyles and enhancing our experience of the world. While we cannot force people to be happy, we have the skills in the built environment professions to design and deliver places that can encourage this. By combining those skills with other professions, such as health and psychology, we can deliver places where people will thrive and prosper and reach their maximum potential. The world is an exciting place—let us also make it a joyful one!

NOTES

1 Hunt, Tristram, "Past Masters", *The Guardian*, 2 June 2004.

2 Department of Communities and Local Government, "Definition of a 'sustainable community'", available at "http://www.communities.gov.uk/communities/sustainablecommunities/whatis/" http://www.communities.gov.uk/communities/sustainablecommunities/whatis/

3 United Nations "Universal Declaration on Human Rights", adopted and proclaimed by General Assembly resolution 217 A (III) of 10 December 1948; United Nations, "Declaration of the Rights of the Child", Proclaimed by General Assembly resolution 1386 (XIV) of 20 November 1959.

4 "Declaration of the Rights of the Child".

5 Maslov, AH, "A Theory of Human Motivation", *Psychological Review* 50, 1943, pp. 370–396.

6 For further information about Bellenden, see English Partnership's Urban Design Compendium 2 "Delivering Quality Places", or visit the website at "http://www.urbandesigncompendium.com/bellendenrenewalarealondon" http://www.urbandesigncompendium.com/bellendenrenewalarealondon

A HAPPY AGE
(BEFORE THE DAYS OF ARCHITECTS)
JEREMY TILL

Recently a local kid glued up our gate lock. I chased him into the housing estate that he lived in, only to be rounded on by his parents who accused me of everything from paedophilia upwards. The hoodies on this estate have especial disdain for cyclists, so on occasions we have been bombed with bags of water thrown down from the sixth floor access balconies as we shoot down the hill. The local police describe the estate as a no-go-zone. This social demise is reflected in the physical decay of the 1960s buildings; as neglected as their tenants, the blocks are now scheduled for demolition less than 40 years after they were put up. A fresh start needs to be made, and new blocks are now being erected around the old ones, and in a complex logistical operation the tenants are gradually being decanted from old to new. Same hoodies, same glue lockers, same water bombers, but new apartments, as if the fresh white spaces will at a stroke cleanse the social ills, as if the architecture will suddenly redeem the tenants, maybe even make them happy. It is at the moment that the old is crashing down, as the new buildings emerge from the piles of rubble, that this equation (fresh architecture=fresh hope) feels so fragile.

What this moment of equilibrium (of old balancing against the new) evokes most clearly is a sense of hopelessness— that this is just an instant in an inevitable cycle of renewal and decay, social and physical, in which the relationship between architecture and happiness is less enduring and certain than the fresh moment of the new might suggest. This short essay explores exactly that gap between the hope and the reality—the hope attached to isolated new architectural beginnings, and the reality of being placed within a much more complex continuum.

FALSE OPTIMISM

Daniel Libeskind, famous for his angular 'iconic' buildings such as the Jewish Museum in Berlin and Imperial War Museum in Salford, always reminds us that architects are inherently optimistic. Where a photographer might depict grief, a poet evoke sadness, a novelist describe anguish, it would be a strange architect indeed who deliberately set out to inflict misery on the world, or who designed a project that purposely made the world a worse place. Architects attach to their projects the hope that they will transform lives for the better. In the most insistent versions of joining hope to stuff, it is implied that architecture is not just a necessary condition for happiness but a sufficient one, as if architecture alone provides conditions for betterment. It is as if we actually believe Le Corbusier's pronouncement that: "there does exist this thing called architecture... a product of happy peoples and a thing which in itself produces happy peoples. The happy towns are those that have an architecture."[1] It is that 'in itself' that is so telling about Corbusier's polemic on the heroic potential of architecture—and it must be a polemic because it takes only a glance out of any window to understand that the hope of a direct, instrumental, link between architecture and good mood is specious. Of course, architecture contributes to mood, both good and bad, but it is part of a much wider set of social and personal forces, most of which are beyond the direct control of the architect. It is exactly this lack of control that makes the architect feel so uncomfortable, and to escape this uncertainty the tendency is to invest all one's hope in things that one can control—proportions, tectonics, materials, form—hence the refinement and polishing of architecture as a set of purified objects that presume to escape dependency on those other forces. For this reason, as Libeskind's recent work—more angular and visually excessive than ever—shows only too clearly, architectural optimism is all attached to a reading of architecture as aesthetic and symbol, and the more 'radical' the nature of the aesthetic or form, the higher the implied level of optimism that something new is happening.

HOPELESS BEAUTY

The prime architectural means of delivery of this happiness is that of beauty. The association of beauty with happiness is one of those platitudes that have been passed unthinkingly from one architectural generation to another. By the time that the baton reaches the writer, Alain de Botton, the association is stretched to breaking point as he struggles to

sustain such a simple, simplistic, idea over the length of his book Architecture and Happiness. But at least de Botton's approach is benign enough in its replacement of architectural ego with a gentle rumination on nice spaces that make one feel good. More worrying is when the association of beauty to happiness is asserted as an inviolate truth. Thus the modernist architect Walter Gropius writes: "in a long life I have become increasingly aware of the fact that the creation and love of beauty not only enrich man with a great measure of happiness but also bring forth ethical powers".[2] Beauty, and beauty alone, here has the miraculous power to redeem, providing happiness at a personal level and ethical behaviour at a collective level.

Gropius is far from alone among architects, ancient and modern, in making the claim that aesthetics and ethics are mutually dependent; that a good aesthetic, in the form of beauty, leads directly to a good life, in the form of an ethical society, and equally that an ethical society is the necessary context for the context of good aesthetics.

Housing demolition and construction,
North Road, London.

This closed loop is very consoling for architects, because it places them—as arbiters and purveyors of aesthetics—as central figures in the ethical process and in the production of happiness. Architects here enter into a comfort zone in which they believe that they are doing good by doing what they do best, namely making beautiful things. The founding of architectural optimism on the *beauty=happiness* equation makes absolute sense within this comfort zone, but with a closer inspection, that simple association begins to unravel. Most poignant of all is the great sociologist Zygmunt Bauman's argument that "the greatest crimes *against* humanity (and *by* humanity) have been perpetrated in the name of the rule of reason, of better order, of greater happiness".[3] It is under the guise of the promise of happiness that the more ruthless aspects of modernity are tolerated. Beauty and happiness are here not benign qualities best appreciated by the bourgeois aesthete and comfortable intellectual of de Botton's pages, but are the cover for the insistent execution of power and control. "Beauty, alongside happiness, has been one of the most exciting promises and guiding ideals of the restless modern spirit", writes Bauman.[4] Beauty and happiness are bound to the notion that conditions—architectural and societal—can be transformed into perfected states through the exercise of control and expertise. Beauty—as exemplified in the

aesthetic catchwords of order, harmony and proportion—
is the handmaiden of the much wider project of modernity—
the execution of order, social norms and reason, a project
that Bauman has so brilliantly shown is hardly one of
benign objectivity.[5]

MAXIMUM HAPPINESS

Architecture thus becomes one of the most powerful
mechanisms in the delivery of the *promise* of happiness on
which modernity is founded. Modernity offers the continual
assurance of something better; progress is the headlong
rush towards that promise. Beyond moments of intimacy
and love, modern happiness lies neither in the present, nor
in de Botton's wistful reminiscences of the past, but in the
expectation of an unknown but hope-fully improved future.
This is why Bauman argues that: "happiness was bound
to remain a postulate and an expectation: its fulfilment
a promise always some distance ahead of reality".[6] So if
architecture, as object, is to represent the promise, it can
only do so in distinction from the reality of the delivery
of happiness. The great modernist projects, with all their
utopian drivers, could only ever stand for a better future,
they could never actually provide it in full.

The clients for Park Hill in Sheffield, one of the greatest of
all those projects, appeared to understand that architecture
alone could not bring forth happiness, even though that
appears to have been an aspiration for the project. Park
Hill, planned in the 1950s, was the icon of a hopeful future,
clearing people from slums and placing them in a better
environment, in "streets in the sky". In a fascinating report
written to the Chairman and members of the Sheffield
Housing Management Committee, the author notes:

ALTHOUGH EVERY EFFORT IS MADE TO SETTLE
APPLICANTS IN THE HOUSE AND AREA OF THEIR
CHOICE IT IS CLEARLY IMPOSSIBLE TO SECURE
MAXIMUM HAPPINESS OF EVERYBODY AND THERE IS
ESTABLISHED EVIDENCE FROM PSYCHIATRISTS THAT
IT IS NOT SO MUCH THE DEFECTS AND DE-MERITS OF
THE BUILDING BUT IT IS THE INHERENT TENSIONS OF
THE TENANT THAT LEAD TO DISSATISFACTION IN THE
SMALL NUMBER OF INTRACTABLE CASES. WITH THIS
IN MIND THE SURVEY SHOWS THAT PARK HILL IS A
SATISFACTORY "MACHINE FOR LIVING IN" TO USE
LE CORBUSIER'S PHRASE.[7]

That architecture can only be a 'satisfactory' deliverer of happiness is perhaps a more realistic appraisal of its potential, but even this more modest aspiration can only be achieved if architects shift their attention from static objects to the dynamics of social space. As noted above, architectural optimism is mistakenly attached to buildings as things to be refined and perfected in their form and technique. It is an optimism founded on belief in the power of beauty. However, this optimism is misplaced, because the contemplation of the object beautiful is only found in a state of removal away from the flux of everyday space. Happiness found at a distance is short-lived, an evanescent cloud of escape that is blown away by the first winds of reality. Not only this, but any attempts at complete ordering and control in architecture are bound to fail, as all those things that are suppressed in the depiction of 'timeless' beauty come back to haunt the ideal. Time, users, waste, the unexpected event, dirt, chaos—all these and many more may be banished to the periphery of the artificial stage that a new building erects, but all are waiting in the wings to rush on when the photographer has left. And, of course, in all their social dynamism these things dismissed as mere contingencies overwhelm the static perfection, a mere sandcastle in the face of the waves. And in this, these conditions are revealed not as the contingencies of architecture but its very necessities. Time and users in particular are forces that architecture's optimism must deal with. How often does one have to quote Henri Lefebvre's '"(social) space is a (social) product" to remind architects and their clients that buildings do not 'produce' aesthetic space, but are settings for social space?[8]

GROUNDLESS HOPE
Architecture's offering lies exactly here—in its contribution to the formation of social relations. Buildings affect and effect social relations in the most profound ways, from the very personal (in a phenomenological engagement with stuff, space, light, materials) to the very political (in the way that the dynamics of power are played out in space)—or, to take on the feminist maxim ("the personal is the political") buildings conjoin personal space and political space. In recognition of the role that architecture plays in part of (and it really is only part of) the production of that social space, architects need to face up to the responsibility of affecting the social dynamics of others. This is not about the delivery of happiness, that is too fragile and volatile a term, but about the hope that those social relations might

be that much better. To argue that there is not a direct, causal, link between beauty and happiness, or at a wider level between aesthetics and ethics, is not to argue for the dismissal of the role of aesthetics and tectonics, but to more realistically understand the role they play in the context of the much wider set of social dynamics to which architecture contributes. This effectively relieves the pressure on the design of the perfected object beautiful, and of its reception as the be-all and end-all of architectural culture. By all means craft the building, compose the elevation, worry over the detail, but at the same time see these as just some tasks in service to another. The key social, and thus ethical, responsibility of the architect lies not in the refinement of the building as static visual commodity, but as a contributor to the creation of empowering spatial, and hence social, relationships in the name of others.

The original philosopher of happiness, Lucius Annaeus Seneca, should have the final say in the matter of architecture and happiness. "Believe me", he says, "that was a happy age before the days of architects."[9] His gripe is not with architects *per se*, but with architectural knowledge as a form of detached wisdom, which aims at the "great and exalted". In the place of this aloof intellect, Seneca champions the "nimble and keen" mind "whose gaze is on the ground".[10] The suggestion is that if happiness or, in my construction, hope, is to be found through architecture, a different kind of thinking is required: one full of ingenuity, eyes and feet to the ground rather than raised up with pretensions of detached greatness. Otherwise we will be perpetually guilty as charged by Seneca: "that was a happy age before the days of architects".

NOTES

1 Le Corbusier, *Towards a New Architecture*, London: The Architectural Press, 1946, p. 19.

2 Gropius, Walter, *Apollo in the Democracy: The Cultural Obligation of the Architect*, New York: McGraw-Hill, 1968, p. 36.

3 Bauman, Zygmunt, *Postmodern Ethics*, Oxford: Blackwell, 1993, p. 238.

4 Bauman, Zygmunt, *Wasted Lives*, Cambridge: Polity Press, 2004, p. 113.

5 See Bauman, Zygmunt, *Modernity and Ambivalence*, Cambridge: Polity Press, 1991, and still more chillingly, Bauman's *Modernity and the Holocaust*, Cambridge: Polity Press, 1989.

6 Bauman, Zygmunt, *Society Under Siege*, Cambridge: Polity Press, 2002, p. 140. Chapter Four of this book traces the 'history' of happiness from Seneca to present day.

7 I am indebted to the Swedish artist Annika Eriksson for showing me this extract (the emphasis is mine). Annika's brilliant performance/video on Park Hill, entitled *Maximum Happiness* ,was shown at the Sheffield Art 08 exhibition.

8 Lefebre, Henri, *The Production of Space*, trans., Nicholson-Smith, D, Oxford: Blackwell, 1991, p. 21.

9 Seneca, Lucius, *Moral Epistles*, trans., Gummere, R, Vol. 2, Loeb Classical Library, Cambridge: Harvard University Press, 1917, p. 399.

Seneca's dialogue on happiness is *De Vita Beata* "On Happy Life".

10 Seneca, Lucius, *Moral Epistles.*

ODILE DECQ'S
HAPPY PLACE

Paul Virilio, the French cultural theorist and urbanist, said once to his students at Ecole Spéciale d'Architecture in Paris that we have left the time of the functionalistic approach to abstract rationalism of the first part of the twentieth century, and the time of focusing only on the social and quantitative requirements of an emerging new society that was current in the second half of the twentieth century. Today, architects have to face the question of multiple desire, together with the individual's demand for pleasure and leisure.

Functions and social needs remain the first basic tasks of architects, but the question of desire is more complex. Every proposal has to be specific and unique. Nothing can be considered as definitive, every solution is transitory.

The horizon is, by its nature, unreachable. You always travel towards it, and when traveling on the sea you also negotiate with the natural factors and elements. Facing the challenge expressed by Virilio, new horizon lines of architecture are diverse and often contradictory: the urban context of desire versus the cities' density and pollution; the growth of the number of rich people versus increasing social issues of poverty; people's mobility and lightness of construction versus energy saving; space transparency, fluidity and porosity versus walls, frontiers and security; fast communication and exchanges versus local human and direct eye contact.

Facing our world today, I, personally, don't believe in a general and common condition for happiness. As architects, we can propose quiet, relaxed and comfortable places. As people, we can smile when we look at, and live in our buildings. But I can't believe we can provide happiness through architecture. This is too much of a human feeling, which depends on our personal life history. It can't be quantified or estimated depending on what we earn. Architecture can provide a number of conditions for wellbeing. But happiness remains an individual and relative condition. To be able to think that architecture can provide happiness frightens me. It makes me feel that I am becoming authoritative if I try to define what happiness should be for everybody, without any distinction between individuals.

I propose for your smile my housing project in Florence, Italy, that I call "Red lace" or my "girly project" because of the red lace that we, as women, all know men love! It is a housing building under construction in an area called Novoli, close to the city centre. The Red lace is a grid where plants will grow during spring and summer, and flower in red to provide shadow to the south loggia facade, whereas in winter, without the flowers, the loggia will be sunny and warm.

Following pages Red Lace Housing Project, Florence.

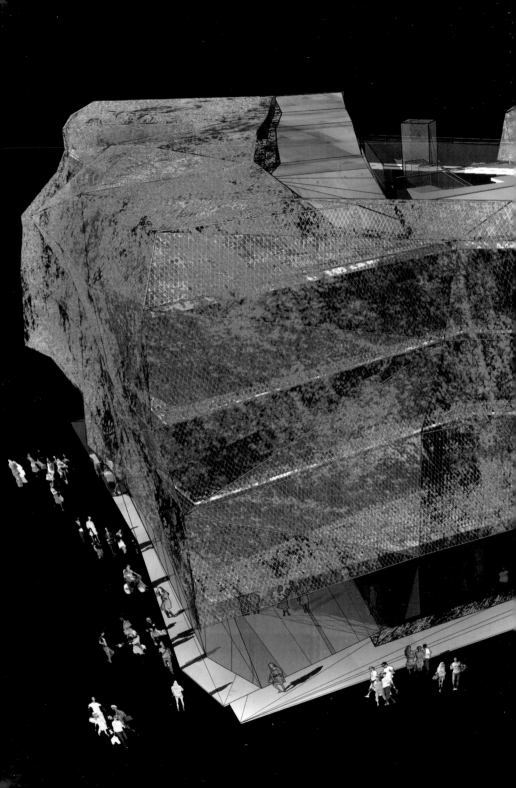

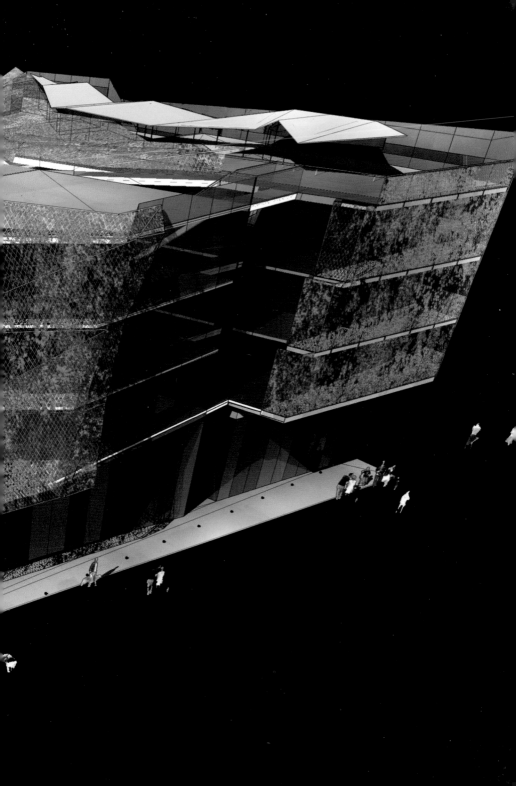

HAPPINESS IN THE LANDSCAPE

MARTHA SCHWARTZ

Let me just start by saying that it is not a prerequisite that landscapes make people happy. There is a time and place for this, and it is the job of the designer to figure out what is being called for and whether 'happy' is an appropriate response. A landscape can make us feel many things, just as a play or movie or painting can evoke a variety of emotions. Additionally, if the designer's intention is to make art (art generally being provocative), then one may find oneself in a place where one does feel provoked—which is not necessarily a happy feeling.

Assuming we do want happiness in the built environment— what then? It's an impossible task to have landscapes that generate 'happiness' in and of themselves, since only people—and not plants—can be happy. Instead, one must imagine the situations that might be conducive to experiences of happiness.

This is a complicated problem. Happiness is a by-product of numerous human emotions triggered by the convergence of many things: a sense of security and belonging, an association of pleasant memories, a connection to the past and to the place, a 'positive' (of course, relative and subjective) aesthetic where one feels uplifted, a sense of possibility and openness, and an impression of choice.

Given the broad intangibles that govern these feelings in each individual—intangibles rooted in complex fundamentals that go way beyond what a landscape can offer (i.e., family upbringing, social expectations, degree of education, political environments, health/economic conditions)—it is clearly impossible for any single entity, even one as large as a landscape, to definitively produce generalised happiness.

The flip side to this is that often, landscapes can bring about happiness through the unsigned and inadvertent spaces that no one has tried to address. One can find happiness in the sheer physical beauty of a leaf or in the reflected glimpse of a cute boy at a suburban mall.

Going back, however, to the issue of design (since that is my profession), I do believe that one can create the possibility of happiness. I would, however, like to clarify that, when designing spaces, my own objectives aim for slightly different targets than happiness. As I have mentioned before, not *all* landscapes call for the creation of *happiness*—some need to be dark, some provocative, some silly or aggressive. Some are surreal or ridiculous.

My goals in designing a landscape centre around reminding us of our surroundings: I want people to think, to stop and ponder, to generate a memory, to develop a reaction, or to simply see anew a place that has dropped out of our view....

I believe that a sense of connection to one another is fundamental to happiness. Even if that connection is a painful one and therefore not 'happy', we value the feeling that we are not alone. The sense of community is fundamental to our mental health, and, ultimately, if one does feel connected to family, to community and to a wider world, the propensity for *happiness* is better enabled.

In landscape terms, I believe that the broader environment must provide a variety of experiences to satisfy any single person. Variety, choice and breadth of these experiences can promote a sense of openness, the freedom to choose different environments according to one's mood or needs. *One* space, or *one type* of space cannot adequately serve a community or even a single person. One must also choose to be in a place if it is not to be a prison.

For example, a Londoner may be very happy to be living in a city like London that can display such fanfare as a Trafalgar Square, replete with history, modern art and civic pomp, and yet, at the end of the week, prefer hanging out with their friends in Clerkenwell Green while having a pint. Both of these types of spaces, one highly contrived and formal, the other a space that has simply evolved over time and is very much about a 'place', can contribute to this person's wellbeing, sense of community, pride in place and therefore *happiness*.

Now for my *own* happiness. The *happiness* I feel has to do with a number of factors: being in an environment that has a strong aesthetic, is visually interesting to me, is full of possibilities and conducive to activities that I like to do. The places that do this for me are often associated with past use and with enjoying myself in some way.

I believe that places where people feel happy are related to aesthetics and, perhaps even more importantly, memory. In looking back upon my favourite places, it's clear that most of them are places where I have had numerous pleasant experiences in a beautiful setting. In fact, I would have to say that the experiences weigh in as heavily as the aesthetics. Of course there's a bit of a chicken-and-egg game here. Usually, *if* I am attracted to a space, I will visit it repeatedly, building up layers of experiences that underpin and enrich my initial appreciation. Every time I re-visit these special places, my sensation of happiness deepens because of both of these things: my increasing layers of positive memories and the continuous beauty of the place.

Beauty does not necessarily depend upon serious design. I know some very humble spaces which make me *happy* every time I visit. These tend to be coloured by pleasant memories and associations, along with a beautiful (though not necessarily magnificent) surrounding.

Given a choice between my childhood backyard and the Grand Canyon, the *happiness* measure would have to go to my backyard. The Grand Canyon is sublime. I am thrilled (thrill not necessarily equaling happiness) to see it each time I visit, but the depth of my experience developed by playing in my own yard wins hands down in the search for a *happy* and emotive place.

Others in the *humble but happy* category include:

VOLLRATH BOWL IN SHEBOYGAN, WISCONSIN

Vollrath Bowl, in the small lakeside town of Sheboygan, Wisconsin, is a huge, terraced earth-formed bowl that rolls down about nine metres, resolving at its end in a children's zoo. It functions as the outdoor living room for the community. At high school commencement, it seats every member of every graduating class, and on the fourth of July, it accommodates the entire town population. It is interesting spatially and sculpturally as it sits there begging children to play on it and roll down its terraces.

For me, as a child, it was an endless source of amusement and play. In the eyes of a small girl the scale of it was huge. Vollrath Bowl is a big, saturnine, child-magnet. We inevitably stained all of our clothing during the rolling, but even today the coolness and smell of crushed grass reminds me of early mornings, feeling giddy and light-headed, and being a young girl.

THE "CONCERT SHELL", INTERLOCHEN, MICHIGAN

The "Concert Shell" exists only in my memory now, as it was recently 'renovated', the magic removed as it stepped up to becoming "a respectable venue for listening to music". However, it remains intact in my memory and provides a place of refuge whenever I have to get my blood drawn or have any other uncomfortable thing done to my body.

The Concert Shell is simply a natural bowl set on the side of a sandy hillside next to a lake. The actual band shell in which a student orchestra played nightly sits at the bottom of the hillside, so that you can watch the concert and the setting sun at the same time. The hillside is forested in mature pines and the sandy ground heavily littered with pine needles. Under and within the trees are long wooden park benches painted in bad peeling forest green. These benches are scattered helter-skelter under and around the trees and rest irregularly on the forest floor. You can view the orchestra through the tree trunks. As the music is playing, the sun sets. Bats jerk and swoop amongst the trees and I make plans to get the cute German trumpet player to talk to me and then get him over to "Date Gate"....

THE SANDWICH BOARDWALK, SANDWICH, MASSACHUSETTS

I have been walking out to the ocean on this boardwalk for 30 years. Every time I walk on it, it makes me feel happy. There is a combination of things that work for me. The boardwalk itself is a miracle—a straight wooden structure that travels over the marshland for almost 244 metres. It makes a beeline to the coastal dunes, crossing over runnels and grooves worn into the mud by the tide. It has no railings and is a good one metre from the top of the mud flats and marsh grasses. There is always the possibility of falling off into the goo, so there is the potential for disaster. You really do have to walk carefully lest you miss your step and fall.

Additionally, the space around you is open and expansive; within one's view-shed, there are very few houses and

buildings to set the tone—you are thrust out there. It is as if you are suspended in mid-air, floating across the marsh grasses like a fly or a bee. At high tide on a summer's night, you can see the phosphorescent plankton in the water. As if that weren't enough, this place is full of the ghosts of the English settlers who built the first boardwalk and used it to gather the white sand for their glass factory.

GRAND AND HAPPY

Ultimately, what makes me happy is to find beauty in a landscape. However, I want to emphasise that beauty can come in many forms: it is not only an aesthetic quality. An idea can be beautiful; sadness or longing can also be beautiful. An idea that is pure and elegant can make me feel very happy. But unless I am actively *feeling* something a place simply doesn't register.

Park Sceaux, south of Paris.

PARK SCEAUX, SOUTH OF PARIS

The first time I ever saw an image of Park Sceaux, I was sitting in Dan Kiley's studio in Vermont in the late 1970s. Flipping through photographs of this baroque garden by Andre Le Notre, I decided right then and there that landscape architecture could be a cool thing to do. This landscape looked to be a mind-blowing, architectonic space of gigantic proportions, made entirely from living materials. I visited this park in 1977 and have since then often returned, watching the park in its phases of full maturity, decay and rebirth. Whenever I walk through Park Sceaux, I am *thrilled* and *happy*. These are two different emotions, but in this place, for me, they fuse.

The heroic physicality of the spaces and beauty of the environment is almost too much for me to take. I am always emotionally spent after having visited the place. However, the layers of memories of this place—of picnics with lovers, husbands, children and friends in this cathedral of space, are some of the most cherished and happy times in my life.

Please scatter my ashes here at Park Sceaux. That would make me happy.

DEYAN SUDJIC'S
HAPPY PLACE

A Boeing 747 is not, conventionally, regarded as architecture.
Yet with its remarkable form, shaped by the demands of
aeronautical engineering pushing to extract the last ounce of
performance from every rivet, panel, and flap, it is undeniably
beautiful. And it is much more than a mute object: it has
spatial qualities. But our view of it has been transformed, now
that we have convinced ourselves that we are destroying
the planet by continuing to use it as thoughtlessly as a bus.
And even the most hopelessly dysfunctional binge flyer will
have noticed that the glamour of flight is not quite what
it was. Business Class on some airlines has produced a cabin
floor plan that looks worryingly reminiscent of the layout of an
eighteenth century slave ship with those would be masters of
the universe packed nose to tail.

But as a hopelessly dysfunctional binge flyer, I have to come clean and confess that there are few things that give a moment of ineffable calm and peace to match the instant that the cabin door finally clicks shut, the captain is cleared for take off, and you know that you have an uninterrupted 12 hours to Bangkok, and another ten on to Melbourne. Savour it while it lasts: inflight wifi is coming. But for now, it is the moment when the accumulated stress of the journey to the airport dissolves, and you are ready to find yourself cloudspotting, thinking about the world, and focussing on the brilliance of the engineers in Seattle who made it all possible.

Following pages Boeing 747 ready for take-off.

DEYAN SUDJIC'S HAPPY PLACE

A CONVERSATION
WITH RICHARD WENTWORTH

On 25 February 2007 Richard had a conversation with Jane
Wernick and Ed Blake in which they explored his ideas about
the city, about how the city reflects our society, and how
the way in which we relate to the physical world affects our
happiness. This is an edited version of that conversation. The
starting point for his thoughts was a recent walk....

Richard Wentworth On a walk in Camden Town yesterday I
was railing against the landscape. We were just walking up
Malden Road. It was just fabulous, and you think how did
London get to be like this? The road is basically the river
Fleet. How did it get to be so torn?

We ended up in Parkhill Road. I was looking for Mondrian,
but I was so busy talking that I missed it. So I ended right
back onto Haverstock Hill, disappointed. I pointed to the
block that faces Parkhill Road, a 1930s block, and said, "If
you don't know who Mondrian is, he kind of set that running.
This is the beginning of Champagne Modernism."

ON COINCIDENCE AND RECOGNITION

Recognition and acknowledgement are the same word. So
that the 'know' and the 'cog' are the same thing. If you don't
have recognition in its fullest sense then you are not very
happy. Nobody likes being cut (in the old sense) in the street.
It is not all 'love me, love me' that we want. It is just like
we need to reassure ourselves—"I am here." Our language
is full of these very physical terms. You can say someone is
a "bit lost", or you can say "if only they were a bit more
grounded". I love that.

We passed the house where Henry Moore lived at the
beginning of the war and I curtsied. One of the people
in the group giggled and said, "My parents live there."
Unbelievable! So in a way it is that same thing, in that we
need these little things, these little bits of friction which
are sympathetic. And now I discover that Jane grew up
in the Mall Studios which was also used by Henry Moore,
Ben Nicholson, and Barbara Hepworth's sister... all that
coincidence in the sediment.

I think if the city is working well for you, if London is
working well for you, this is what it does.

Jane Wernick Shall we talk a little bit about humour?

ON THE PAVEMENT AND SHARED SPACE

RW Yes. One of the things that came up yesterday is that if
you are going to cope with the city, or cope with your own
body in space, then you have to have a sense of humour.
Of course, we talked about the dropped banana skin, the
Tati-ness of it all.

At one point we were a crowd, a gentrifying crowd, half way
up Southampton Road way, and so we completely blocked the
pavement, and a man appeared. He sort of did a wonderful
fish job through the crowd. He didn't say anything, he didn't
go "Excuse me!" which he could have done. But the event was
incredibly eloquent about a collective understanding of what
the pavement is. Of course, the pavement is actually not really
very old : it used just to be the road. And then there was this
invention : "Excuse me, we are pedestrians. You are traffic."

... There was this lovely moment where he negotiated us and
we were somehow an embodied group for that brief moment.
And we withdrew and gave him the space, and there was a
sort of collective smile about what had happened, and we
even felt that he somehow felt that that was odd. But the
pavement is intensely private and beautifully public and you
have odd moments of feeling invaded on the pavement.

During the walk, the mood, as it always does in London,
especially if you are in the company of other people, moved
a lot. So, by the time we had got to the Mall Studios it had
acquired a gentle intimacy.

And the exteriority of the main road, which requires the raising
of your voice to project further little kinds of aggression.... In
fact when I ended my talk on the corner of Parkhill Road and
Haverstock Hill, I was really bellowing. It is good to recognise
that urban range, from too nice to too horrible!

ON OWNERSHIP OF SPACE, AND THE
ANONYMOUS BRICK

I asked if anybody knew how to lay a brick, and there was a sort
of giggle. There were two people in the group who could....

I said I thought what is interesting about the art of brick laying is its anonymity, and that the brick is the greatest single form in the city, and it is never credited to anyone. You see brick laying done well, and you see it done less well. It can never be done that badly because the wall wouldn't stand up, but there is a range of how well it is done. And sometimes you see the piece work—you can see not only the day rates, but also who did each bit—"There's Charlie's work, there's Fred's work."

A woman in our group said "... and it's political". It is political because you are immediately saying "ownership, separation, mine, thine, us, them, whatever", and the brick even embodies that as a form. So you get a rather special moment between the gorgeousness of knowing how to do it, and the physical barrier. In fact there is always a barrier unless there is an opening. No human can walk through a brick wall. It's why we like cartoons.

ON WALKING

The American author Rebecca Solnit writes well about walking. She talks about walking as turning one leg into a column, and then you swing the other one—the one that is not the column. And it becomes a column. It is the fact that humans are forward people, in the sense that we have an arse and a back. And that is why we walked to the top of the hill, although we could have turned back. And there was a very particular sense of achievement. The ground was rising. I suppose we were, in effect, on the edge of the Fleet, the early Fleet, the buried Fleet....

ON MODERNISM AND OLD THINGS, AND THE COMFORT WE GET FROM OLD THINGS

If you were born when I was born—mid-twentieth century— you sort of know the long drawn out British nineteenth century grinding towards some kind of modernity, scraping past Modernism. I have an American friend who talked about how they had Jewish friends in the 1950s around Washington, where everything had to be new. That was because the past was so awful that it had to be not there. So that comes into ideas about American painting, the sheer, "I'm here and it's new!" which we certainly never felt. I grew up in the "Let's convert a redundant building" period. Make do and mend!

Steven Witherford, the other day, said something about embodied wealth or embodied value, "Well, look, somebody

put it here. It is a lot of stuff, and it was put here for various reasons. Let's celebrate their mercantile energy." And there is a kind of, "hang on a moment! Why would you necessarily demolish it?" But then there is the other side of it which makes me feel pretty sick, which is the inappropriate moment. For example there is a house at the bottom of Fitzjohns Avenue, which is everything that saddens me. It has a blue plaque. It is a sort of Norman Shaw-ish, 1905, handsome, confident building, and there is nothing there at all—just a front, and just a blue plaque. It is the most disgusting piece of theatre.

ON THE KERB AND FALLING OFF IT AND WHITE PAINT
You need verticalness to have your confidence to be you, and to be independent. And I think that has fantastically deep metaphors for being a baby, and for being an aged wreck.

Opposite and above Photographs along a walk.

I misjudged a kerb in Rome a couple of years ago and lay on my back in the road. The traffic drove round me! Nothing broken, but an assault on the able bodied system. An obvious metaphor for architecture here.

JW I think reticence can be quite good, because you know, you do sometimes get real joy from discovering something round the corner, something that you don't see at first or that you suddenly see in a different light, or view.

RW There were about 25 of us on the walk, and there was a temptation to say, "we have come to buy your house", or to pretend we were a religious thing. People were looking out of windows. It was a Sunday afternoon, and I was saying, "you can make these houses look...", and I was talking about white paint, and how there was no white paint until Bridget Riley existed. The chemistry of white paint is an early 1960s thing. I imagine there is a point at which munitions production goes down and white paint production starts to go up.

Well, they would have been painted with that distemper, not oil-based paint, because anything oil-based always went to that wonderful cream colour that we grew up with. So, I was just talking about whiteness, and how London used not to be so white. And there was a house on the East side of Malden Road, which is opposite the 70s block, which has patches of render and faded blue paint. And I was saying to everyone, "That's what London looked like in the 70s and the 60s." Queensgate looked like that. Nottinghill looked like that. And I said, "Then it started to be held together by Dulux which is really not more than 15 years ago." And, actually, it is a micron of nothing that makes it look prosperous, but it is nothing more than a t-shirt. Nothing.

ON COMMUNITY
I said "Does anyone here use the word 'community'?" Somebody said "I do", without any irony, and, of course, I wanted to lie on the floor and laugh, because what is 'community'? You know the three of us formed a small community here 20 minutes ago, and if you have got one in here (points to his head and immediate surroundings) you do not need to use that word. You only use it in Britain if you feel threatened. And how strange that is. But actually if we were in France the word would embody the parish or the commune. It is a different kind of allegiance, and we don't have that here.

The parish must have been amazing. Bollards are the last vestige of that. They have the language on them. We are living in the last period when they are markers of the public good. And they (parishes) were a force for the public good. We were also talking about all this ridiculous public space that is neither public nor private, and how people nominate it. We were passing this 70s block, and there was this building that had on it the Camden Council's green sign, with four white buttons covering up the screw caps. It read, "Headcorn". I said, "Where would you get a name like that?", but it was sort of rhetorical. But there was somebody walking with us who lives on Prince of Wales Road, and she said, "We don't call it Headcorn. We call it the block over the chemist." And I just wanted to hug her because she could speak for the experience, and I could speak for the speculation about the experience.

ON GENTRIFICATION

Let's talk about Jerry White's book, *London in the Twentieth Century*. I would love to meet him. His description of gentrification (which is us) is so rich and so complex. It describes how different people are motivated and how the city didn't really become self-conscious/managed until the early 1970s. And he described the eruption of estate agents, (the 'Prebbles' and the 'Stickley and Kents'). It is very eloquent, and he talks about how attitudes towards migrations, or anything else that we are going through now, all happened during the First War, such as big anti-Semitic stuff—"There are too many of them, and they are all in Cable Street." It really reads like it was in the *Daily Mail* yesterday. And the Germans who lived in London, a lot of whom lived in Belsize Park. The Germans were a very important part of a kind of community. That, I think, is important for your emotional fabric. I do not want to be with lots of people who are quite like me, which is why I have never desired one of those amusing little places off Kensington Church Street.

JW I get the impression that, for you, what makes you happy in the built environment is richness of one sort or another.

RW ... and argument. Such as with the shops along here, (Hackney Road) where there are the last, pitiful remnants of the Hoxton spindlers, next to the "we'll unblock your mobile phone" shops. And that migratory thing I enjoy—why did that happen, when did that happen? How was it permissioned?

JW Like waves of migration and then you get the debris of the wave....

RW Which is very good in Jonathan Raban's *Soft City* a chapter called "The painted Moroccan Birdcage" about the first time those shops appeared in places like Maida Vale. They were opened by hippies who liked birdcages and sold them. And this created a sort of pointless commerce. It is incredibly eloquent. The fripperies of commerce and taste.

ED BLAKE Some of what you say conflicts with some of the findings...for example in David Halpern's book, *More Than Bricks and Mortar*, he talks about mixed communities having high rates of certain mental health problems... so the idea that "richness necessarily equals happiness" is problematic.

RW The richness... I've had years when I've earned minus money. But we are able to make choices and you can test it in your own relationships. You know that you have seen people go to the wall in one way or another,... but actually we go for no more complexity than we find amusing. That is a harsh way of putting it, but if we find it too complicated, or if the Caledonian Road got too much more like it already is, I can move. There is no hiding the privilege of what I am saying about us.

I have always found it amusing that I live ten or 11 doors from the Caledonian Road. That is a really good distance.

The comings and goings of start-up small enterprises is a cruel thing. When we were in Morgan Road yesterday we saw something called "Pristine Dry Cleaners", which I thought projected that they were pristine. A great brand name, but quite a cheap Londoners' joke.

ON COMPLEXITY

There was that sense of being in a very fragmented place, and the little girl, the daughter of the lady who made the 'Headcorn' observation, was talking about her school, and I could feel that she was saying that it was too complicated.

The mum also said that it is well too complicated here. She was referring to the cultural mix. She was ironic, but in a wonderful old London Way. There is point on that road where there is an end of block, and there is wall here and maybe a bin space, a steel door and a pole here. But then, looking

at a lot of sculpture and painting, and being completely
pretensious about it I said, "please notice the delicate
arrangement of the angle and the point of contact with
the blank rectangle". It was a tease about the American,
formalist art critic Clement Greenberg The mum said wryly,
"Yes, you mean it's yob proof." She was talking about the
streets at night. She was talking about lost-ness and the
feeling of predatory.

JW If you could do something to a part of London to make
people happier what would that be?

RW It would be growing things.... It would be growing things....
The sight of Hyde Park as a cornfield or something.... It could
be economic... that is what could be so interesting about it. I
think we are living in a place which is fantastically responsive
to husbandry. If we had that relationship with our city perhaps
we would be happier. And I like that word (growing) anyway...
feeling that you are engaged with that process...

JW There is also research that says, if you see greenery
on your way to work your levels of depression are
significantly reduced.

RW Well that says something about the high footfalls in the
places which aren't really the parks, but they are the greens....

AND FINALLY, ABOUT GOOD DIMENSIONS
RW... things like enjoying door width, and stairs.... God,
stairs.... Just imagine if we had an edict that all stairs had
to be beautiful body voyages!—You know: The pleasure of
going down a good set of stairs...The pleasure of going up a
good set of stairs.... The ghastliness of going down a bad set
of stairs. In a way all of architecture is a stair: rising, pace,
conduct. Walking with someone up a set of stairs can be
quite a pleasurable, processional thing....

... Wouldn't it be great if children were really taught how
pleasurable dimensions can be, if you get them right?
A brick is the size of a brick because you can pick it up...

And so the conversation continued....

DAVID LAN'S
HAPPY PLACE

One of the best ideas hard-wired into the new Young Vic
theatre is the way the office areas embrace the auditorium,
wrapping around it three layers of warmly protective
corridors. Everyone who works here can't help but feel in
their bodies their relationship to the purpose of this place:
the shows we make here.

The highest refinement of this idea is the way a door out of
my office dovetails precisely to a door into the auditorium
at the highest level, directly onto the technical gallery. This
allows the following: I sit working at my desk. Over the
show relay I hear the sound of laughter from the auditorium.
Within seconds I'm in the gallery gazing down over the
audience. If I am really quick I'm there before the smiles on
their faces fade away.

Laughter is the best sound you can hear in a theatre. It is
most likely to happen between friends. A theatre building
is most successful when it creates an easy sense of social
promiscuity: a bunch of strangers will have an intense
collective experience, perhaps hang around for a while and
then go home. Its design must dissolve the ritual barriers we
anxiously maintain between self and stranger. Think of the
intensely non-convivial proximity of the economy carriage
of an aeroplane. You can't enjoy a show with that amount of
tension in the air.

You certainly laugh more easily if the theatre feels full. Design
can help here too. Theatres with designated seats, if they're
not packed, leave acres of emptiness between the high price

and the cheap ones, generating anxiety. "Oh my god, I should have believed the reviews, stayed in and watched telly." If people can choose where to sit they tend to gather, forming the confident front that allows relaxation and pleasure. Theatre needs to create a circle of complicity. Everyone who happens to be in that room at that moment, actors and audience, hold metaphoric hands as newfound friends.

There is another level of laughter in the Young Vic too, one not quite so generous. Built to last five years in 1970, it was, by 2000, in chronic disrepair. We worked for some years with our wise and intuitive architects Haworth Tompkins and their attendant teams, raised bagfulls of cash, struggled and cursed our way through a two year wrestle with our contractors, opened on time and budget and won a handful of awards. Not long before the end we learned that, before the rebuild began, the Arts Council, our major funder, had come to the view that "if a bulldozer drove down The Cut and destroyed the building for good, no-one would shed a tear". The stone the mason rejected has become the chief corner stone. Or to put it another way: Ha ha ha!

As I write this I'm watching a member of my technical team sitting out on the terrace in the spring sun eating her supper salad with a grin—what put it on her face I don't know. My office is so designed that as I work I can look down into our cafe on mezzanine and ground levels and out into the street, all alive with people of every age, size, hue drinking and eating. A soft fruity buzz rises up to me on this blissfully warm evening. As soon as I finish this paragraph, I'll go out of my office through the dovetailing door and onto the technical gallery to watch the audience flow in for the preview of a new show. As it happens, the house will be full. If this isn't happiness in the built environment, what is?

Following pages
Left The Young Vic Theatre auditorium.
Right Looking into the foyer.

CAN URBAN TOPOLOGIES
PROMOTE
HAPPINESS?

TAMSIE THOMSON

Over the last hundred years philosophers, architects, researchers and sociologists have struggled to prove what most of us feel instinctively, that our urban environment has an effect on the human psyche and that this in turn has an impact on our happiness. The link, while at once so instinctive to the lay person, has been difficult to prove in any conclusive way. It is this struggle and the debate that surrounds this subject which I hope this book has helped to inform. The discussion among architects and planners about the effect of the built environment is not new, and this essay takes a look at the work of a number of the key thinkers in the field.

The need for this 'happy society' can be seen in the ongoing debate surrounding sustainable communities and more finely in the discussion around high density living. "For any tower block to work reasonably well as a community the flats need to be let to people who are content to be there."[1] While this seems like common sense it is a principle which has struggled to be achieved in any city or neighbourhood. This is not for want of trying. Since the Renaissance, we have been trying to make idealised cities but the resulting quality testifies to how little we understand the nature of urbanity, or perhaps it is simply how little we understand urbanity's impact on us. With the benefit of hindsight we are able to judge the performance of past typologies and perhaps begin to understand our relationship with the urban.

This instinctive feeling that there is a link between urban surroundings and our happiness is fed by the human need to embellish, adorn and modify our physical surroundings. Humans since the dawn of time have made 'persistent attempts to mould the material world to graceful ends. People have strained their backs carving flowers into roof beams and their eyesight embroidering animals onto tablecloths. They have given up weekends to hide unsightly cables behind ledges.[2] This impulse to beautify must have some reward, that of providing pleasure to the inhabitant, or it would seem a fruitless enterprise. We feel that our surroundings can affect our state of mind, that they convey messages. This belief has led to the suggestion that if buildings have meaning then this meaning can affect our own psyches and beliefs.

Collective studies including those by Gillis in 1977 in Canada, Edwards also in Canada in 1982 and Bryne in 1986 found that environments can become stigmatised and this can have a measurable and considerable impact on the residents who live in them.[3] If this symbology can affect us negatively then it also has the power to act as a positive force. Neils Gutschow, in his paper on Kaunas in Lithuania describes how the building of a hydro-electric dam became a symbol of hope and happiness in the city despite its almost immediate redundancy.[4] If by symbolism alone buildings and urban typologies can so profoundly affect our mental states, what might be the outcome of their direct impact on our daily life through design interventions and decisions?

There is some evidence that certain types of mental illness, such as depression, may be lower in rural communities than in cities.[5] As Alain De Botton in his book *The Architecture of Happiness* writes "Taking architecture seriously therefore makes some singular and strenuous demands upon us.... It means conceding that we are inconveniently vulnerable to the colour of our wallpaper and that our sense of purpose may be derailed by an unfortunate bedspread."[6] The National Tower Block Network in their 1992 report identified isolation and depression as a problem associated with tower blocks.[7] Of course, people feel depressed and isolated across the globe in many types of cities and buildings, but if we can prove that certain built forms have particular effects on our psyche or happiness then it must be crucial that we design out these effects.

This goal is perhaps most succinctly summed up in the discussion around modernism and its particular urban typologies. It is modernist blocks which seem to have been most blamed for betraying their inhabitants in cities across the world. Camillo Sitte is credited with being one of the originators of the idea that the new 'modern' approaches to city planning may be adversely affecting the city's inhabitants (as well as its artistic ideals). In his treatise

City Planning According to Artistic Principles, written in 1889, he prophesied that the new 'modernist' planning would create a city where "genius is strangled to death and *joi de vivre* stifled by the system."[8] He was writing this as a rebuke to the 'modernist' developments in Vienna at a time of economic growth and housing shortage. His arguments were countered by Otto Wagner, an ardent believer in the redemptive nature of modernism. Both men wished to create "a new aesthetic of city building in which social aims were influenced by psychological considerations".[9] Against the uniform grid Sitte proposed the free forms of the ancient street pattern, as he felt that its picturesque historicism was psychologically satisfying and that the open boulevards and large blocks advocated by Wagner would create agoraphobia in the city dweller. Wagner's ideals were expanded, perhaps most famously, by Le Corbusier in his 1929 book *The City of Tomorrow* where he advocates this modern functional city as a way of achieving happiness. "In seeking happiness, we should strive towards a sense of equilibrium. Equilibrium means calm, a mastery of the means at our disposal, clear vision, order, the satisfaction of the mind."[10] It was this vision of the future which was pursued by planners across the globe, particularly to address the problems caused by the post-war housing shortage throughout Europe. Adolf Abel, a professor in planning at Munich Polytechnic, published a book in 1950 called the *Regeneration of Towns* in which he stated that "The ideal schemes are like poetry, made from men's happiness."[11] These proposals were all strongly linked to the growing functionalist movement that had its roots in the teachings of Wagner. In his book *Die Stadt von Morgen* Karl Otto used this philosophy as a way of creating "a city that would provide happiness to all".[12] His city provided a functionality he believed was lacking in the old historical centres, while providing a utopia for a happy society. There were criticisms, however, that this functionalist city did not respect the way that people wanted to live their lives.

By the 1960s the voracity of these claims was being strenuously refuted even in countries within the USSR, where such designs had become the norm and dissent was repressed. In Joze Bevc's1963 film *Citizen Urban* devoted to Ljubljana, Slovenia portrays the central character 'Urban' being removed

Man sunbathing.

from his apartment in the old city centre and moved into a skyscraper on a new housing estate. The film follows him as he deals with his dislocation and disorientation before finding happiness surrounded by his old possessions back in the historic centre.[13] As with Sitte the link is made between the 'modern functional' city and unhappiness. It is this vision of a rational world, a departure of historical forms which has been held responsible for the problems associated with post-war planning. Le Corbusier has been blamed for much of the unhappiness and social malaise witnessed on twentieth century housing estates. This sentiment is summed up by De Botton

HE (LE CORBUSIER) FORGOT, THAT WHILE THERE IS MUCH TO HATE ABOUT SLUMS, ONE THING WE DON'T MIND ABOUT THEM IS THEIR STREET PLAN.... THERE IS SOMETHING ENERVATING ABOUT A LANDSCAPE NEITHER FREE OF BUILDINGS NOR TIGHTLY COMPACTED, BUT LITTERED WITH TOWERS DISTRIBUTED WITHOUT RESPECT FOR EDGES OR LINES, A LANDSCAPE WHICH DENIES US THE TRUE PLEASURE OF NATURE OR URBANISATION. AND BECAUSE SUCH AN ENVIRONMENT IS UNCOMFORTABLE, THERE IS ALWAYS A GREATER RISK THAT PEOPLE WILL RESPOND ABUSIVELY TO IT, THAT THEY WILL COME TO THE RAGGED PATCHES OF EARTH BETWEEN THEIR TOWERS AND URINATE ON TYRES, BURN CARS, INJECT DRUGS—AND EXPRESS ALL THE DARKER SIDES OF THEIR NATURE AGAINST WHICH THE SCENERY CAN MOUNT NO PROTEST.

The belief in the radiant city to improve happiness had begun to be questioned by evidence of the social decay in most examples. However, instead of questioning the typology there was a rejection amongst planners of what was termed "determinism", that the environment may in some way shape our behaviour. Instead there was a belief in what Alice Coleman called "possibilism" that people were good or happy regardless of environment or typologies.[15] A great deal of research has been conducted to prove that this link does exist and to revaluate our understanding of determinism, a limited number of which are discussed below.

In 1939 Faris and Dunham published a study of the geographical distribution of the home addresses of persons admitted for psychiatric disorders in Chicago. They discovered that the pattern of psychiatric admissions across the city was far from even: the psychiatric admission rate was the lowest in the outer suburbs and became steadily higher towards the inner city core. Faris and Dunham argued that the isolation and disorganisation of the inner-city led to a social and mental disorganisation of the individuals who lived in those areas, and hence to elevated levels of psychiatric disorders. However, the interpretation of these associations was greatly compromised by the recognition of the occurrence of social selection or drift. People with poorer mental health were less likely to be economically successful and tended to end up living in less pleasant and desirable environments.[16] While it is hard to prove the link between mental illness and the city as a general concept what we can prove is that specific design variables do have a quantifiable effect.

Oscar Newman was at the vanguard of this research with his seminal treatise on defensible space written in 1972. He identified three design factors that directly contributed to crime on particular housing estates. These were anonymity, lack of surveillance and alternative escape routes. Not only did he make the link through his research but also suggests it was causal, by improving one of the variables and then monitoring the resulting drop in crime rates. This research has been followed up by numerous reports and research studies examining the links between happiness, mental health and different design variables. Many of these are listed in Halpern's comprehensive book *More than bricks and Mortar?* Evidence has been found to suggest that excessive heat, the absence of daylight, certain weather patterns and higher levels of air pollution can all have effects on mental health. Evidence for these effects can be found from laboratory studies, community surveys and fluctuations in psychiatric admission rates. In 1990 Alice Coleman conducted research on whether different design typologies had an effect on what she termed social malaise. She surveyed 4,099 blocks and some 100,000 dwellings in the UK against these indicators of malaise which were litter, graffiti, damage, children in care, urine and faeces. While her terminology is different from that of happiness, it is reasonable to deduce that if one is happy with one's environment one does not participate in the behaviour described here. Coleman was trying to establish whether certain design features were causal in this behaviour. What she discovered was that when other variables such as poverty and unemployment were removed, there was a direct link between instances of malaise and certain design variables. The strongest links were building size, number of dwellings sharing an entrance, number of storeys in the block, overhead walkways, confused public private space

and number of blocks per site.[17] Many of these factors have been suggested by other studies, and one that has received particular attention is the impact of the design on social interaction and how this makes people feel 'happy' about their environment. Studies by Frank in 1983, Lefebvre in 1984 and Willmot in 1963 have all found that the larger the number of dwellings in a development, the lower the number of neighbours that are known and the lower the level of attachment to the community.[18] This means that it is possible for the built environment to facilitate supportive patterns of neighbouring.[19] There are many examples of how the design of houses, developments and cities have significant and demonstrable effects on the behaviour and wellbeing of the people who live in them.[20] However, most of the example listed are most commonly seen in the large housing estates and urban topographies associated with modernism or the functionalist movement. If, as Church and Gale believe,

"sustainability must ultimately be judged through the experience of residents", the sustainability of this typology must be called into question.[21] As Coleman puts it "Designs which have this disadvantaging effect are an iniquitous imposition upon people who cannot cope with them."[22]

Considering the need to promote happiness through architecture or urban design presents designers, government and civil society at large with a problem. But, despite its ethereal nature, happiness must again become a focus for city design, because the consequences of not considering it are immense. There are many other concealed costs traceable to faulty housing design, arising from social breakdown, such as the medical costs of treating people suffering from mental illness, of people unable to work, of the disturbance of child rearing practice and the cost of repairing the damage to the building caused by this 'social malaise'.[23] "A stable, sustainable community cannot be built where people feel negative and are looking to leave."[24] It has been argued that the highest rates of psychiatric admissions are associated with areas that are poor, high in density, mixed in land use, and associated with other types of social disorder such as social delinquency, suicide and crime. If we know that "human behaviour tends to deteriorate under the stress of inappropriate habitats", we must question the viability of these new communities.[25]

If a typology can make "even mature adults feel, think and act differently", then imagine the results if we were able to harness this power to improve society's happiness.[26] Indeed perhaps, as De Botton provocatively puts it, "a beautiful building could reinforce our resolve to be good".[27] So, if we were to be more prosaic perhaps we should start by not reproducing typologies we know to be harmful, whilst not forgetting the aims of the past to create a utopia. It may be that research on the scale of the Coleman project needs to be undertaken to identify typologies and features which will create positive feelings within ourselves.

There have been some 'utopias' or attempts to create general happiness which have proved to be more successful. The English New Towns are examples where studies have

Girl skipping.

found that the overall effect of New Towns is to produce slight improvements in physical health.[28] While this is not radical there have been some experimental communities which have expanded upon this through the garden suburb model. The most famous of these is Bedford Park, London which was built in the words of its creators as a model of the "capitalistic communal" in the pursuit of 'corporate happiness' and by all accounts for a lengthy period it was very successful.[29] "The usual suburb was monotonous in appearance and dull to live in; Bedford Park was interesting to look at and apparently fascinating to live in."[30] There have been reasons given for the success of this utopia, not least the fact that its occupants were self selecting and socially homogeneous, but there are some factors that the typology and architecture allow, namely that each resident was able to control their own territory, that the design of the dwellings was flexible, and people were allowed to make requests about the specifications.

We have seen how buildings can affect people's behaviour and their sense of happiness but we are still creatures of individual free will. A number of surveys have shown that attachment to the neighbourhood and the quality of the relationship with neighbours explain to a large degree the variation in residential satisfaction. If, however, a person (in the same area) is not in frequent social contact with their neighbours, then the objective quality of the dwelling makes a very large difference to residential satisfaction. In other words, residents who are involved in their local community tend to be happy with where they live regardless of the physical quality of their homes.[31] It is most likely that typology as a factor in our happiness is what Coleman describes as 'probabilism', that it is on a sliding scale where the 'worse' the typology becomes the more it affects people adversely.[32] We know that few people really consider architecture, but many people are instinctively affected by it. We must never lose sight of this or the huge responsibility that this places on designers.

NOTES

1 Church & Gale, p. 6.
2 De Botton, p. 15.
3 Halpern, p. 155.
4 Gutschow p. 91.
5 Halpern, p. 16.
6 De Botton, p. 25.
7 Church & Gale, p. 9.
8 Sitte.
9 Schorske, p. 62.
10 Le Corbusier, p. 40.
11 Bergeijk, p. 326.
12 Bergeijk, p. 321.
13 Azman, p. 209.
14 De Botton, p. 246.
15 Coleman, p. 20.
16 Halpern, p. 11.
17 Coleman.
18 Halpern, p. 121.
19 Halpern, p. 123.
20 Halpern, p. 211.
21 Church & Gale, p. 15.
22 Coleman, p. 3.
23 Coleman, p. 171.
24 Church & Gale, p. 6.
25 Coleman, p. 170.
26 Day, p. 7.
27 De Botton, p. 117.
28 Halpern, p. 16.
29 Bolsterli, p. 12.
30 Bolsterli, p. 10.
31 Halpern, p. 113.
32 Coleman, p. 20.

REFERENCES

Azman, Lucka, "Citizen Urban, the search for happiness" in Wagenaar, Cor, ed., Happy: Cities and Public Happiness in Post-War Europe, Rotterdam: NAI Publishers, 2000.

Bergeijk, Herman van, "Thomas Wech's Spiritual Town Planning" in Wagenaar, Cor, ed., Happy: Cities and Public Happiness in Post-War Europe, Rotterdam: NAI Publishers, 2000.

Carl, Peter, "Cities and the Pursuit of Happiness", Icon, November 2004.

Church, Chris and Toby Gale, Streets in the Sky; Towards Improving the Quality of Life in Tower Blocks, London: National Sustainable Tower Blocks Initiative, 2000.

Clark, Ross "Ugly Buildings Don' t Kill People", The Times, 8 February, 2007.

Coleman, Alice, Utopia on Trial; Visioning and reality in planned housing, London: Hilary Shipman, 1990.

Day, Christopher, Places of the Soul; Architecture and Environmental Design as a Healing Art, London: Thorsons, 1990.

De Botton, Alain, The Architecture of Happiness, London: Hamish Hamilton, 2006.

Gutschow, Niels, "Happiness in the Light. The Construction of a New Power Plant in Kaunas, Lithuania 1959" in Wagenaar, Cor, ed., Happy: Cities and Public Happiness in Post-War Europe, Rotterdam, NAI Publishers, 2000.

Halpern, David, More than Bricks and Mortar; mental Health and the built Environment, Abingdon: Taylor and Francis, 1995.

Jacobs, Jane, The Death and Life of Great American Cities; The failure of town planning, New York: The Modern Library, 1961.

Jones Bolsterli, Margaret, The Early Community at Bedford Park; The Pursuit of "Corporate Happiness" in the First Garden Suburb, London: Routledge and Kegan Paul, 1977.

Layard, Richard, Happiness; Lessons from a New Science Harmondsworth: Penguin, 2005.

Provoost, Michelle, "Happy Hoogvliet" in Wagenaar, Cor, ed., Happy: Cities and Public Happiness in Post-War Europe, Rotterdam: NAI Publishers, 2000.

Sampson R and W Groves, "Community Structure and Crime: Testing Social-disorganisation Theory", American Journal of Sociology, 94, 1989, pp. 774–802.

Schorske, Carl E, Fin-De-Siecle: Politics and Culture, New York: Random House, 1980.

Sitte, Camillo, City Planning According to Artistic Principles (1889) trans. George R Collins and Christiane Crasemann Collins, London: Phaidon Press, 1965.

Wagenaar, Cor, ed., Happy: Cities and Public Happiness in Post-War Europe, NAI Publishers, 2000.

JANE WERNICK'S
HAPPY PLACE

The Royal Botanic Gardens at Kew has long been a favourite place to visit, with its extensive gardens, full of interesting trees and plants, and its collection of beautiful glasshouses. It appeals to serious botanists, lovers of architecture and structure and those who just want a peaceful place to walk or have a picnic. Recently Kew has been continuing the Victorian tradition of building projects that are embedded in the park, and for me, one of the happiest is the Xstrata Treetop walkway which provides a 180 metre long stroll through the deciduous trees originally laid out by Capability Brown, at a height above ground of 18 metres.

As others have mentioned, one's feeling of happiness in a particular place will usually be the result of a number of factors. So for me, leaning against the handrail a couple of Sundays ago, my pleasure probably came as much from knowing that I had had a hand in its design, and hearing all the good comments around me, as from the built object itself. The project, the brainchild of Kew's head arboriculturalist Tony Kirkham, aimed to engender a greater love of trees amongst young people, and an understanding of how important they are to our planet. I am sure this will happen. With such an enthusiastic client, and a equally committed team of architect and builder (Britland Steel) we had just come to the end of one of our happiest projects.

As well as being educational the project is also about producing a feeling of delight, which is a constant aim of the architects, Marks Barfield. This is achieved firstly by bringing us up high amongst the branches, into a position that we very rarely occupy, surrounded by nature, yet with views of elegant buildings such as the temperate house, and the longer sights of London that provide orientation and anchor us to our city. At the same time, the structure itself gives delight—It sits well amongst the trees, with the tapering pylons, which divide into three even more slender branches.

The walkway itself is composed of simple trusses, with a seemingly random, yet deliberate arrangement of slender diagonals, clad with an almost transparent mesh. Walking through the boughs of the trees brings back chidlhood memories of tree climbing and clamboring through hedges. The weathering steel provides a variable rusty surface in a rich orangey-brown that blends well with the greens and brown of nature.

The slenderness of the pylons, which were designed to be strong enough under the most extreme loads, matches that of the trees. Yet the trees sway further in the wind being of timber rather than the stiffer material of steel. Never-the-less the walkway does sway a little, which gives a small echo of the rocking you would get in a tree house.

Following pages The Xstrata Treetop walkway, The Royal Botanic Gardens at Kew.

BIOGRAPHIES

WILL ALSOP
Will Alsop is an architect based in London. He is responsible for several distinctive and controversial contemporary buildings, most in the United Kingdom. Alsop's work is usually distinguished by its vibrant use of bright colour and unusual forms. He has also held several academic posts, including tutor of sculpture at Central Saint Martins College of Art and Design in London

ED BLAKE
Ed Blake is a trainee architect based in London. He is also an architectural researcher based at Building Futures, at the RIBA. His research interests include happiness and conflict in architecture.

KEITH BRADLEY
Keith Bradley is an architect based in London. He is a senior partner at FeildenCleggBradley Studios and runs their London office. His work has an emphasis on urban regeneration. He is also a member of the CABE National Design Review Panel.

ODILE DECQ
Odile Decq is an architect based in Paris. She has worked on various projects, including public housing, a campus library and a boat. She is a Member of the French Architecture Academy and a *Chevalier de la Légion d'Honneur.* She is also an RIBA International Fellow.

POORAN DESAI
Pooran Desai is sustainable entrepreneur based in London. He helped found the sustainable community development company BioRegional Quintain where he is Sustainability Director. Pooran studied physiological sciences at Oxford University. With architect Bill Dunster he initiated the BedZED eco-village. He is also Technical Director of the international "One Planet Living" initiative.

ROS DIAMOND
Ros Diamond is an architect based in London. She is the founder of Diamond Architects. She has taught at the Architectural Association, Oxford Brookes School of Architecture and the Bartlett. She has also co-edited a number of books on architecture and is an editor of the architectural journal *9H*.

MAX FORDHAM
Max Fordham is a building services engineer based in London. He founded Max Fordham LLP in 1966, and is one of the UK's foremost authorities on environmentally friendly engineering. He studied physics at Cambridge before completing a postgraduate engineering conversion course. He was President of the Institution of Building Services Engineers, 2001–2002, and awarded their gold medal for services to engineering in 1997.

ANTONY GORMLEY
Antony Gormley is a sculptor based in London. Over the last 25 years Antony

Gormley has revitalised the human image in sculpture through a radical investigation of the body as a place of memory and transformation, using his own body as subject, tool and material.

DR HILARY GUITE

Hilary Guite trained as a medical doctor initially working in medical oncology and later training in general practice in London's East End. She then retrained in public health medicine. She works part-time for Greenwich Teaching Primary Care Trust on a range of public mental health topics, including the impact of the physical environment on mental health. She is now working on public health aspects of mental health promotion and mental health services.

DAVID HALPERN

David Halpern currently works in the Institute of Government, London. He has previously worked at the Prime Minister's Strategy Unit as a policy advisor and Chief Analyst. He has written several books, including *More than Bricks and Mortar: Mental Health and the Built Environment*.

LOUIS HELLMAN

Louis Hellman is a cartoonist based in London. He studied architecture at UCL and the Ecole des Beaux Arts, Paris. He has worked as an architect and since 1967 as a cartoonist featured in trade, national and international print, including *The Architects'*

Journal, *Building Design* and the *RIBA Journal*. He has also lectured extensively.

SIMON HENLEY

Simon Henley is an architect based in London. He combines practice with teaching, writing and research, and is the author of a recently published book on multi-storey car parks. Simon has taught at the Bartlett, amongst other teaching roles. In 2002 he was short listed for Corus "Young Architect of the Year". He is member of the NHS Design Review Panel, and the CABE School Design Review Panel.

DAVID LAN

David Lan is currently Artistic Director of the Young Vic, London. He trained as a Social Anthropologist at the LSE. After two years of field research in the Zambezi Valley, he was awarded a PhD for a thesis on religion and politics. He led the rebuild of the Young Vic theatre and the two year Walkabout season while the theatre was closed.

BYRON MIKELLIDES

Byron Mikellides is an architectural academic based in Oxford. He is Professor of Architectural Psychology in the Department of Architecture at Oxford Brookes University. Specialising in the psychology of architecture, he is the author of several books, including *Colour for Architecture*, with Tom Porter.

HUGH PEARMAN

Hugh Pearman is currently editor of the *RIBA Journal*, based in London. He started his career as a reporter on *Building Design* in the 1970s and has worked across various architectural titles and national newspapers, including 20 years at *The Sunday Times*. He is also author of several books on architecture.

RICHARD ROGERS

Richard Rogers is an architect based in London. He is the senior partner in Rogers Stirk and Harbour. His early work includes the Pompidou Centre, Paris and the Lloyds Building, London. Recently, he designed Terminal 5 at Heathrow. He is the winner of the Pritzker Architecture Prize, and the recipient of the prestigious RIBA Gold Medal.

MARTHA SCHWARTZ

Martha Schwartz is a landscape architect based in Cambridge, Massachusetts and London. Her projects range from the private to those at an urban scale. She became Professor of Landscape Architecture at Harvard University Graduate School of Design in 1992. She has served as a visiting critic at many universities. Schwartz recently established a second firm in London.

PAUL SMITH

Paul Smith is a fashion designer based in London. He is primarily known for his menswear, but covers the whole spectrum of fashion design. He is credited with introducing a number of trends within contemporary fashion and 'lifestyle', including the revival of boxer shorts and of the Filofax.

DEYAN SUDJIC

Deyan Sudjic is the Director of the Design Museum, London. Before moving to his post at the Design Museum, he was the design and architecture critic for *The Observer*, the Dean of the faculty of Art, Design and Architecture at Kingston University, and co-Chair of the Urban Age Advisory board.

JEREMY TILL

Jeremy Till has a dual life as architect and educator, based in Sheffield and London. He is a partner in Sarah Wigglesworth architects and Dean of the School of Architecture at Westminster University. He is also author of several books on the subject, including *Echo City*.

TAMSIE THOMSON

Tamsie Thomson is the manager of Building Futures and an architectural tutor based in London. She has a background in architecture and an MA in Housing from Edinburgh College of Art, with a specialism in housing design and ethnic diversity. She then went on to work for the Civic Trust and the charity Shelter. After gaining her MSc in Urban Design, Tamsie joined Building Futures in 2005 and is responsible for the overall management of the group, its staff, members and projects.

SARAH TOY

Sarah Toy is a chartered civil engineer, based in London. Her initial focus was on working with local communities to provide low cost water and sanitation facilities in Africa and South-East Asia. The aim of her work is to deliver appropriate infrastructure through cross-sectoral approaches, which she sees as central to securing sustainable public health and wellbeing benefits for society.

LORNA WALKER

Lorna Walker is a London-based environmental engineer and a CABE commisioner. She is managing director of Lorna Walker Consulting. Amongst her many other roles she is a Visiting Professor for the Royal Academy of Engineering, at the University of Sheffield. She was a Director of Ove Arup & Partners and the leader of Arup Environmental. She was also a member of the government's Urban Task Force.

KIRSTY WARK

Kirsty Wark is a journalist and television presenter based in Glasgow and London. She is best known for fronting BBC Two's news and current affairs programme *Newsnight* and its weekly arts annex *Newsnight Review*.

RICHARD WENTWORTH

Richard Wentworth is an artist based in Oxford and London. He is also a curator and teacher currently working at the Ruskin School of Drawing and Fine Art in Oxford.

He is identified with the New British Sculpture movement of the late 1970s. Having taught at Goldsmiths College his influence can be seen in the work of the Young British Artists.

JANE WERNICK

Jane Wernick is a structural engineer based in London. She has specialised in the design of structures which play a large role in the total architecture of the building. She was Principal in Charge of Ove Arup & Partners' Los Angeles office and an Associate Director of Ove Arup & Partners. She is now Director of Jane Wernick Associates Ltd.

ACKNOWLEDGEMENTS

This book would not have happened without the RIBA Building Futures group. It is chaired by Dickon Robinson. A past Director of the Peabody Trust, and a CABE Commissioner for many years, he continues to advise on many aspects of architecture, urbanism, sustainability and regeneration. In his role of Chairman he has given continuous, generous and critical advice throughout this project. Building Futures is managed at the RIBA by Tamsie Thomson, who believed in the significance of the Happiness project from its beginning in early 2007. She has done an amazing job in organising the seminars and debates, and in making it possible for this book to be realised. She has been tirelessly assisted by Ed Blake who has been undertaking research, tracking down photographs, providing editorial assistance and generally helping in his role as Project Coordinator.

The Building Futures Steering Group whose members include architects, academics, developers, researchers and engineers, has proved to be a fantastic source of encouragement, contacts and ideas.

I have been privileged to work with all the contributors. The range of conversations we have had prove that this is a topic that will provide food for thought for many years to come. It has been a great subject to discuss because it is almost impossible to do so without smiling.

Finally, I must thank my office for accepting, uncomplainingly, the time that the Happiness project has taken from the practice.

To find out more about the work of Building Futures please visit www.buildingfutures.org.uk

Images used by kind permission of Amos Goldreich, Antony Gormley, BBC, Bioregional, Drax Power Ltd, Getty Images, HBG Construction, Jane Wernick, Jeremy Till, Jose Lasheras, Martha Schwartz, Louis Hellman, Odile Decq, Peter Cook, Philip Vile, Pooran Desai, RIBApix, Richard Bloomfield, Richard Wentworth, Simon Doling, Tim Soar, Will Alsop and Yutaka Saito.

pp. 8, 12–13 All images courtesy Jane Wernick.
p. 9 Image courtesy Man-Cho Choi.
p. 22 Image courtesy Jane Wernick.
p. 23 Above Image courtesy Oundle School.
p. 23 Below Image courtesy Tim Soar.
pp. 24–29 Images courtesy Peter Cook, Jose Casheras, Amos Goldreich.
pp. 32–33 Image copyright BBC.
pp. 36–37 Image courtesy O'Donnell + Toumey.
pp. 42–43 Image courtesy and copyright Yutaka Saito.
p. 45 Image: Ed Blake, reproduced from Cities for a Small Planet.
p. 47 Image courtesy Pooran Desai.
pp. 54–55 Image courtesy Richard Bloomfield, Flint Photos.
p. 57 Image: Harold M Lambert.
Image courtesy of Hulton Archive, Getty.
p. 61 Image: David Sutherland.
Image courtesy Photographer's Choice, Getty.
pp. 68–69 Image: Alastair Hunter.
Image courtesy RIBA Library Photographs Collection.
pp. 78–79 Images: Ed Blake.
pp. 84–85 Image courtesy Drax Power Ltd.
pp. 88–89, 92-93 Image: Bill Toomey.
Image courtesy RIBA Library Photographs Collection.
pp. 100–101 Image courtesy Will Alsop.
p. 104 Images: Ed Blake, reproduced from Guite and Toy.
p. 108 Image: Ed Blake. Reproduced from Guite and Toy.
pp. 114–115 Image courtesy Richard Bryant, Arcade.
p. 115 Image courtesy Matt Gray, Digital Vision, Getty.
pp. 124–125 Image courtesy Jeremy Till.
p. 130 Image: ODBC.
pp. 142–143 Image courtesy Ken Reed, Stone and Getty.
pp. 146–147 Images courtesy Richard Wentworth.
pp. 154–155 Images courtesy Philip Vile.
pp. 158–159 Image courtesy Emmrich-Webb, Stone and Getty.
pp. 162–163 Image courtesy Richard Kolker, Photographer's Choice, Getty.
pp. 168–169 Images courtesy Jane Wernick.

Other Building Futures publications include

The Building Futures Game: Developing Shared Visions for Neighbourhoods

Living with Water: Visions of a Flooded Future

Housing Futures 2024: A Provocative Look at Future Trends in Housing

21st Century Schools: Learning Environments for the Future

21st Century Libraries: Changing Forms, Changing Futures

The Professional Choice: The Future of Built Environment Professions

COLOPHON

© 2008 Black Dog Publishing Limited, London, UK,
Building Futures and the authors, photographers, artists
and architects.
All rights reserved.

Black Dog Publishing Limited
10A Acton Street
London WC1X 9NG
info@blackdogonline.com

Cover image courtesy Retrofile RF Getty.
Photographer: George Marks.

Designed by Emily Chicken at Black Dog Publishing.

All opinions expressed within this publication are those of
the authors and not necessarily of the publisher.

British Library Cataloguing-in-Publication Data. A CIP
record for this book is available from the British Library
ISBN 978 1 906155 469

All rights reserved. No part of this publication may be
reproduced, stored in a retrieval system, or transmitted,
in any form or by any means, electronic, mechanical,
photocopying, recording, or otherwise, without prior
permission of the publisher.

Every effort has been made to trace the copyright holders,
but if any have been inadvertently overlooked, the necessary
arrangements will be made at the first opportunity.

Black Dog Publishing Limited, London, UK, is an
environmentally responsible company. *Building Happiness*
is printed on MultiArt Silk, FSC certified, an FSC
certified paper.